BEYOND DESPAIR

BEYOND DESPAIR

AHARON APPELFELD

THREE LECTURES

AND A CONVERSATION WITH PHILIP ROTH

TRANSLATED

BY JEFFREY M. GREEN

FROMM INTERNATIONAL

PUBLISHING CORPORATION

NEW YORK

Printed in the United States of America.
First U.S. Edition

1 3 5 4 2

Library of Congress Cataloging-in-Publication Data
Appelfeld, Aharon.
  Beyond despair : three lectures and a conversation with Philip
Roth / Aharon Appelfeld ; translated by Jeffrey M. Green. — 1st
U.S. ed.
      p.   cm.
  ISBN 0-88064-150-9 (alk. paper) : $17.50
  1. Holocaust, Jewish (1939–1945), in literature. 2. Holocaust,
–Sources. 4. Holocaust, Jewish (1939–1945)—Influence.
5. Appelfeld, Aharon—Interviews. 6. Authors, Israeli—Interviews.
I. Roth, Philip. II. Title.
PN56.H55A65   1994
809'.93358—dc20
                                              93-34763
                                              CIP

IN MEMORY OF MY PARENTS
BUNYA AND MICHAEL APPELFELD

THE 1991 RADOV LECTURES

Center for Israel and Jewish Studies
Columbia University

The Radov lectures are
a biennial series
established through the generosity of
Sylvia and Joseph Radov
of Winnetka, Illinois.
The purpose of the endowment
is to bring
to Columbia University
distinguished figures
in the realms
of Jewish scholarship, thought,
and literature.

CONTENTS

INTRODUCTION

The three lectures presented here took shape within me over the past years. They do not present an organized body of thought, but rather reflections and feelings grounded in the tribulations of a Holocaust childhood, wanderings and displacement across the ruins of Europe after the Second World War—and a belated childhood in Israel. I have tried to avoid abstractions and to connect my reflections to things seen. Vision, meaning also color, scent, and sound, is the most faithful emissary of memory. I said "memory," and I immediately retract it. Anyone who underwent the Holocaust will be as wary of memory as of fire. For many years the members of my generation were concerned with the concealment and repression, or, to use a harsher word, the suppression of memory. It was impossible to live after the Holocaust except by silencing memory. Memory became your enemy. You worked constantly to blunt it, to divert it, and to numb it as one numbs pain. This battle lasted for years. People learned how to live without memory the way one learns to live without a limb of one's body.

In the first lecture I briefly describe life without memory and how memory burst forth from the prison where it had been sent. Now I wish to say a few words about how memory becomes clothed in words. The transition from repressed memory to words arouses suspicion and hesitation. The sights were dreadful and immense, and words are frail and impotent. Life after the Holocaust seemed an untimely resurrection, a new nightmare. No one knew whether this was rescue or punishment. How were you to live from now on? These questions, like memory, became enemies. Everything was so bewildering as to drive you mad. All that you knew, acquired, were told about seemed to nullify itself, and you, too, seemed to nullify yourself.

There was no place for the individual, for his pain and despair, in the camps. No one there said: I have a headache, a toothache, I'm in a bad mood, I'm homesick. In the camps there was no place for a vocabulary with a domestic tone. The individual, or what was left of him, was nullified, and only a barren gaze remained, or, rather, apathy. After the Holocaust as well, there was shame in talking about oneself. The Jewish belief that the world depends upon the individual failed the test. "Death to death," I remember hearing a religious Jewish survivor shout in the midst of the liberation camp. I didn't know what he meant. Now it seems to me that he was referring to the indifference that surrounded the survivors and threatened to submerge them in another death—mute silence.

To write about the Holocaust is impossible, it's forbidden, people said repeatedly, and you agreed with them, for this was also your own feeling. The first writing about the Holocaust was in the documentary style most suitable to journalism in the collective plural. To write about oneself, about one's personal feelings, seemed selfish and vulgar. People fled to the general, to the external, to the social conclusion. The interior was locked away. Even then I noticed: the deepest pains often dress in the most vulgar clothing. The deepest and most delicate feelings were hesitant to stand naked. Many years passed before people dared to raise their tortured lives up from the hidden recesses. Mostly they seemed to remain in the depths. For years I sought a way out, a standpoint from which I could begin to converse with myself. The need to clothe the memory in words grew stronger over the years. My first efforts at writing were some poetry and a chronicle. The poems were no more than stifled screams, shouts for help, and shouts to God. In those gaunt poems was the whine of a lost animal, but beyond that, nothing. In the chronicle I tried to describe what had happened to me after I was separated from my parents. I tried to be faithful to my memory. Memory seemed to be the most necessary content of my experience. To be faithful to what had happened was an imperative from which one was not to deviate. But what was I to do? For memory itself proved to be the enemy of my writing. After I placed it in writing, my childhood experience of the Holocaust, which was in my bones—and even over the distance of years it remains clear and precise—sounded unreliable to me, more like fictional material. Memory, in which I had believed so strongly, had deceived me. I refused to accept that and continued to write, faithful to memory. The result was, among other things, a sentimental, one-dimensional story about a Jewish boy wandering in the woods, nourished by plants and finding shelter with marginal people during the cold seasons. True, it was my childhood story, but what emerged from the writing sounded bizarre, unconvincing, and, even worse, invented.

Compulsive memory took over my writing, denying me access to any other creative element. It took me years to understand that the inner enemy was impeding my writing. The turning point occurred when, in a feeling of despair, at a certain stage I started to write not about myself and about what had happened to me during the Holocaust, but about a Jewish girl wandering in the woods and villages. That would seem to be a trivial change, but miraculously, as though with a magic wand, my compulsive memory was removed, and in its place, or alongside it, came, one after the other: the sense of alternatives, of proportion, the choice of words—all the devices that the artist needs for writing. The question facing me was no longer what happened, but what had to have happened, which is truly the question of every artist. For many years I had been certain that any deviation from memory was sinful. That principle was sacred to many Holocaust survivors, and I followed in their footsteps. Fear of omitting any detail of the full story of suffering—that fear gave them no rest.

While the survivors of the Holocaust were oppressed by memory, other writers, mainly people who had not experienced the dread, tried to write about the Holocaust using their imagination. The results were far worse. If memory binds you to what happened, not permitting you to differentiate between primary and secondary, between private and general, the imagination attracts you to the bizarre, to the exceptional, to the speculative, and—far worse—to the perverted.

It is astounding how easily true life can be falsified when it is clothed in words. There can be no literature without memory, and memory is not only fact and vision and the course plotted for them, but also a warm emotion. Memory is doubtless the essence of creation. But occasionally memory, if one may say so, is also a mass in which important and unimportant things are mingled together, and it demands a dynamic element to make it move and give it wings, and this is what the imagination usually does. The power of the creative imagination does not lie in intensity and exaggeration, as it sometimes seems, but rather in giving a new order to facts; not in inventing new facts, but in their correct order, so that "the idea" of the author is visible. Life in the Holocaust does not demand the invention of new facts and sights. That life was so "rich" one could choke on it. The literary problem is not to pile up fact upon fact, but rather to choose the most necessary ones, the ones that touch the heart of the experience and not its edges.

During the Holocaust there were brave Germans, Ukrainians, and Poles who risked their lives to save Jews. But the Holocaust is not epitomized by the greatness of these marvelous individuals' hearts. What characterizes the Holocaust is the alienation that beset the Jew on every side. It is important to know that there were marvelous individuals and to know that the flame of humanity was not completely extinguished. But one cannot say that the Holocaust revealed man at his most splendid. I say this because survivors sometimes feel deep gratitude to their rescuers and forget that the saviors were few, and those who betrayed Jews to the Nazis were many and evil. Here is another example: In Israel, because of embarrassment at the passivity of the victims, the heroism of the partisans and ghetto rebels has been emphasized. That was the need of the hour, and one can understand it. But what can be done? This emphasis has created a distorted picture, as though the Holocaust were entirely represented by the marvelous heroism of the ghetto rebels and the partisans, who fought for their lives, and as though it had been forgotten that in the Holocaust there were also other kinds of heroism, less splendid, but very human. For example, young people who might have been able to save themselves preferred to accompany their aged parents, staying with them until the last moments of their lives.

Apologetics and glorification always distort. The question is: How are we to return to the individual, in particular during a period when the self was nullified? How do we restore to the individual the humanity and honor of which it was deprived? Without the individual there can be no sentiment and no human warmth. Everything is dragged into great generalizations and abstractions.

Up to now we have subjected the experience of the Holocaust to memory. This was important. Holocaust survivors have created an impressive body of memoirs. Historical research has also produced comprehensive factual material, including the historical, social, and psychological background of the period. Now it seems to me that the time has come to ask ourselves how we are to bring this dreadful experience into the circle of life. Until now we have asked what was the case. From now on we must take the liberty of asking what must have been the case. In other words, we must transmit the dreadful experience from the category of history into that of art.

I began to develop these ideas about literature and the Holocaust when Professor Yitzhak Twersky of Harvard University invited me to speak there in 1980. In their first draft, these lectures were presented at the University of Washington in Seattle in 1985, where I was invited by the Stroum Foundation. At that time I presented a number of ideas which I have developed and expanded over the years. I presented the second lecture in its final form at a 1987 conference in Albany, New York, which dealt with writing and the Holocaust, and it was published in the anthology *Writing and the Holocaust*. I am grateful to Holmes & Meier, the publishers of that volume, for permitting me to reprint it here. I gave the three lectures in their almost final form in 1991 at Columbia University. I am grateful to the Radov

Foundation, which sponsored the lectures, and to the Columbia University Center for Israel and Jewish Studies, and to its director, Yosef Hayim Yerushalmi.

Many people helped me to bring these lectures to their final form. Though I cannot thank all of them by name, I would like to mention my friends Professors Leslie Epstein and Yitzhak Twersky for their constant encouragement and for discussing these ideas with me. Thanks are also due to Joseph Wenkert, who published my first book of essays in Hebrew, *Essays in the First Person*. Many of the ideas included in these lectures were first expressed there.

This volume also includes a comprehensive conversation with my friend Philip Roth, which was published in *The New York Times Book Review* on February 28, 1988. My friendship with him allowed me to tell him things that I had not told other people. Even more, it enabled me to crystallize a number of ideas and sentiments that I had borne with me for a long time. I have devoted most of my writing to stories and novellas. I believed, and I still do believe, that only art has the power of redeeming suffering from the abyss. For years I refrained from any conceptual expression, for I was suspicious of all plural language and all generalization. Philip restored some of my faith in conceptual expression. I had to repeat to myself that conceptual expression also belongs to the vocabulary of human expression, and that we have no choice but to humanize it and refine it, and hence my gratitude to him.

A.A.

LECTURE ONE

LECTURE ONE

I am about to present you with a series of sensations and images, and above all emotions, which molded me and my generation. I do not know how significant my personal remarks will be. My craft, which has kept me at a distance from abstractions, imposes concreteness upon me on this occasion as well. Ever since it became conscious of itself, literature has been taken up with the impossible task of joining the particular with the general. Quite likely my own efforts will also fail to go beyond self-evident failure.

Though I mentioned "emotions," I immediately wish to take that word back. Any emotion, even the clearest, is elusive. You try to touch it, to feel it, and for a moment it seems you have succeeded—but no, it has already slipped away or worse, altered. It is no coincidence that earlier generations within the Jewish tradition attributed little value to emotion. Not that they were unaware of its mastery, its obsessive force—but they did not allow it to be expressed. In a generation where the solid conventions have been destroyed, emotions come to the fore.

I also referred to "my generation." To be more precise, I mean people whose childhood and youth were lost in Europe between 1939 and 1945, the years we call the "Holocaust."

The twenties and thirties saw a great drive towards assimilation. Mass emigration, communism, and inner collapse undermined Eastern European Judaism and threatened to bring it down. Assimilation was everywhere. True, great communities, ancient and deeply rooted ones, still maintained the traditional forms, but more through inertia than inner strength. That was the final, difficult stage in the transition from tribal, religious unity to modern petite bourgeoisie.

The petit-bourgeois spirit gradually engulfed everything, creating a new Jewish mentality, which, it seems to me, has not yet received sufficient attention. Kafka's father, to pick an extreme case, is typical of it. Taken together, the drive to acquire education and property, to fit in and get ahead, overtook the petit-bourgeois Jewish world.

This is how Kafka describes it in his well-known letter to his father:

> It would have been thinkable that we might both have found each other in Judaism or that we even might have begun there in harmony. But what sort of Judaism was it that I got from you? In the course of the years, I have taken roughly three different attitudes towards it.
>
> As a child I reproached myself, in accord with you, for not going to the synagogue often enough, for not fasting, and so on. I thought that in this way I was doing a wrong not to myself but to you, and I was penetrated by a sense of guilt, which was, of course, always ready to hand.
>
> Later, as a young man, I could not understand how, with the insignificant scrap of Judaism you yourself possessed, you could reproach me for not making an effort...to cling to a similar insignificant scrap. It was indeed, so far as I could see, a mere nothing, a joke—not even a joke. Four days a year you

went to the synagogue, where you were, to say the least, closer
to the indifferent than to those who took it seriously, patiently
went through the prayers as a formality, sometimes amazed
me by being able to show me in the prayer book the passage
that was being said at the moment, and for the rest, so long as
I was present in the synagogue (and this was the main thing) I
was allowed to hang about whereever I liked. And so I yawned
and dozed through the many hours (I don't think I was ever
again so bored, except later at dancing lessons) and did my
best to enjoy the few little bits of variety there were, as for
instance when the Ark of the Covenant was opened, which
always reminded me of the shooting galleries where a cup-
board door would open in the same way whenever one hit a
bull's eye; except that there something interesting always
came out and here it was always just the same old dolls without heads. Incidentally, it was also very frightening for me
there, not only... because of all the people one came into close
contact with, but also because you once mentioned in passing
that I too might be called to the Torah. That was something I
dreaded for years. But otherwise I was not fundamentally dis-
turbed in my boredom, unless it was by the *bar mitzvah*, but
that demanded no more than some ridiculous memorizing;
in other words, it led to nothing but some ridiculous passing
of an examination; and so far as you were concerned, by little,
not very significant incidents, as when you were called to the
Torah and passed, in what to my way of feeling was a purely
social event; or when you stayed on in the synagogue for the
prayers for the dead, and I was sent away, which for a long
time—obviously because of the being-sent-away and the lack
of any deeper interest—aroused in me the more or less un-
conscious feeling that something indecent was about to take
place. That's how it was in the synagogue; at home it was, if
possible, even poorer, being confined to the first Seder, which

more and more developed into a farce, with fits of hysterical laughter....This was the religious material that was handed on to me.

(Franz Kafka, *Letter to His Father*)

I chose this passage because I feel it faithfully describes the emptiness of the Jewish petite bourgeoisie, which, from that time to the present, has hardly changed. It is no wonder that sensitive people such as Otto Weininger and Karl Kraus fell victim to self-hatred. Kafka himself, were it not for his delicate sensitivity and his thirst for the root of his existence, would doubtless have followed in their footsteps. Was the Jewish petite bourgeoisie an island surrounded by tranquility and stupidity? Anyone who has lived among them knows that those Jews were worried, panicky, and ambitious, Jews who hid behind a paper mask which could easily be stripped away to reveal their face. Nor let us forget that that milieu also produced the great and impressive Jewish minds which arose during the past hundred years and took Europe by storm, and not just in literature. The Jewish complex—acute sensitivity and broad culture—is not apparently a bad recipe for artistic creativity. But unfortunately, it proved poisonous upon more than one occasion to the individual Jew and to his entire people.

I would like to return to my own life history. I was born in the city of Czernowicz, a city which was very Jewish and also very assimilated, a pleasant city inspired by the spirit of Vienna, since until the First World War the region belonged to the Habsburg Empire. The Jews of Czernowicz wanted very much to be like the Viennese, whose charm so enthralled them that even very sensitive and well-educated people, people with a good degree of self-criticism, unfortunately did not feel that there was anything reprehensible about their self-rejection.

At the outbreak of the Second World War we were children. Our parents were about forty years old. What had we absorbed during those few tranquil years before the war? Nothing, it would seem. But nevertheless, everything was stored up within us. First of all, the family. Through our families we lived in cities and villages, in poor shops and large wholesale outlets. The family is Jewish history writ small. Within it there were the surviving believers, those who still believed out of habit, those who were alienated without realizing it, and those who were consciously alienated. Every phenomenon that had taken place during the past hundred years was represented within the family: there were anarchists, communists, Zionists, and Bundists. And the more extended the family, the deeper were rifts within it.

For my generation, assimilation was no longer a goal, but it had become a way of life, if one may say so. True, a few remnants of Jewish existence still quivered within us, but they were devoid of life. The petit-bourgeois Jew regarded himself as free of the ancient traditions and thus as a potential candidate for big business, medicine, law, and engineering. In the petit-bourgeois manner of thinking, both then and now, there was no serious place for Judaism. Judaism was seen as an anachronism from which it was difficult to free oneself entirely. Our grandfathers still kept the commandments, but they did not have the strength to imbue us with faith. With their own eyes they saw the fall of every barrier. They did not believe they could change a thing. Their sadness, if I felt it correctly, was not that of the aged, but that of the defeated. There were no longer any discussions, arguments, and counter-arguments, only melancholy resignation. There were also a few angry grandfathers, but they aroused nothing in us except what is found in every half-assimilated Jew: hatred for his tradition.

Assimilation had become our heritage by then. No one sought to justify or condemn it. The question of course was simply one of time. But time, in our case, was not generous. The processes of assimilation, which appeared to be marching forward with confidence towards complete integration, were halted by an enormous satanic hand.

The Holocaust which suddenly descended upon us bound us within the depths of suffering without making any distinction between the believer and the alienated. To us children, it was perhaps easier. Our suffering was essentially physical and implied no soul-searching. For our parents it was the loss of a world. All their beliefs were overthrown in a single day. They were left with nothing but their naked Jewishness. The Jewish secret, which no longer existed, or which flickered but faintly, was suddenly stripped of all its garments.

In empty lots, in open railway stations, and in hostile fields stood tens of thousands of Jews, separated from their dear ones, deprived of all their property, stigmatized by shame. All those years they had fled from the Jewish collectivity, because it seemed to them that the ancient heritage hemmed them in and blocked their path to full freedom. Now they were together, Jews from the East and from the West, in the same boat, and under an iron sky.

The terror extended over six straight years—I doubt whether there were ever six such long years in Jewish history. They were years when every minute and second and fraction of a second were laden beyond their capacity. Because that terror extended for so many years, every feeling or thought of ours passed through the refining furnace of suffering.

The Jew suddenly had to confront, against his will, not only the full horror of his existence but also the disintegration of the beliefs which just the day before had given support, structure, and meaning to his life. We discuss the Holocaust in terms of physical suffering without seeing that the spiritual suffering was no less extreme. If from the outside they were assailed by accusations, from within they seethed with spiritual agony. Who and what is a Jew? In the penal colony that distress was their daily bread and water.

Suffering of that sort was not the children's lot, although they absorbed it all in their blind cells, as only children can absorb things. In that turmoil there was no place for words and questions. Therefore they quickly learned not to ask. From silent expressions they learned how to imprison fear. They will never forget their parents' expressions on the empty lots where tens of thousands of people were crowded together. Each one was left to himself. What is one to do? How can one save the children? That was the final love which bore them from place to place. They took limitless risks. We were the meaning of their lives. Even then, hurriedly, in flight, as we saw how they sacrificed themselves to find a safe haven for us, we know that in their self-sacrifice on the brink of the abyss they were bequeathing us not only life but also the ultimate significance of their own existence.

Did they wish to see us continue spinning the thread of denial and hide the trail so that no one would know who or what we were? Or perhaps, when they stood at the brink of the abyss, they had something else in mind.

We try to understand the Holocaust in sociological, political, and sometimes even theological terms. However, it seems to me that the depths of the tragedy cannot be plumbed in the confrontation between victim and murderer, but rather in the bitter fact that most of the Jewish intelligentsia did not view themselves as allied with the Jewish tradition. Satan descended upon that intelligentsia, as in metaphysical dramas, Satan himself, and, without observing any niceties, he brought them, against their will, back to the Jewish collectivity.

People will never forget the astounded expressions of the German and Austrian Jews, most of them assimilated for generations, who were exiled to the ghettos in the East. There they encountered, to their astonishment, the ghetto Jews, Yiddish Jews, whom they had attempted to ignore for so many years. The hand of Satan did what only his hand can do: it brought them to the very place they wished to flee. That encounter with oneself which was imposed upon one, the encounter with everything that just yesterday had seemed anachronistic, idle, old-fashioned, and meaningless to one—that meeting is what forced the commencement of a spiritual accounting which, to this day, has not been brought to its final reckoning.

It is difficult, but one must say so: latent processes of self-destruction accompanied by self-hatred had taken place years before the Holocaust. That was primarily true among the intelligentsia. In the midst of one's march towards the enchanted realms of self-rejection, the satanic hand came and brought one back to the foundations of tribal existence and commanded one to see it through, not as an individual, and not because of one's opinions, but because one was a member of the Jewish people.

Let us, however, return to our experience. Everything was overthrown in a single day. We were first exiled to transit areas and then to the railway stations. In the enormous panic of the crush and hunger, words were lost and thought was erased. Even so, we did manage to absorb our parents' bitter silence before the appearance of the hand that separated us. Our parents protected us until the last minute. When they could no longer do so, they left us, the way Moses' mother left her baby, to the mercy of the heavens.

From then on loneliness was our lot. Some of us were in the forests, some in monasteries, and some with tyrannical peasants, who treated us like beasts. We quickly learned the secret of our Judaism, and that we had to hide it so that no identifying mark was visible on us. Instinct whispered to us that the better we hid it, the greater were our chances of living. A few were lucky.

Thus, with no parents, in enemy fields, isolated from humanity, we grew up like animals: cowed and oppressed by fear. The life instinct guided us, and we obeyed it. In the forests and villages we felt the secret of our Jewishness. It was then, apparently, that the knots were tied which bound us to the flickering flame of the Jewish secret. We knew that that secret made us fair game for every hand and axe, but without it our existence would be more meager. That secret was our only shelter from all our misery. There we hid away our homes and the image of our parents' faces. Sometimes that was the last refuge.

Over the years we learned to live with death as with a familiar acquaintance. Not that we ceased to be afraid of it. On the contrary, every encounter with death increased our fear, but the promise we had given to our parents, that we would look out for ourselves, made us stronger than we were. We wandered from forest to forest, as if we were not children but rather animals who were born in the dark thickets. Here we learned how to get food from the trees, fire from the stones, and to reflect.

Why were we so persecuted? In the woods and on the riverbanks that question appeared in all its nakedness.

Sometimes we were certain that it was our smell, our long ears, fear of darkness. If only we overcame those flaws, no one would guess we were Jews. At that time we did not yet know that that was the old Jewish self-accusation which had been passed on to us like a curse.

Our Jewishness lacked a social background. That is not to say that what we had absorbed at home did not leave any traces, but that what came afterwards effaced our memories of home, it did make them fainter. We always knew that our Jewishness was not only a secret but also a disaster. There were moments when in our hearts we cursed our fate, the fate of the persecuted innocent. Whenever our spirits failed, we also turned our backs to it.

We spent close to three years in the forests. It is strange to say, but now, when we remember them, we feel no bitterness. That was a kind of childhood where reality and legend were mingled, the body got to know the cold of the nights, how to overcome fear, how to get food out of the earth—quite literally. In those years we learned from the trees and the streams. Our parents had left us and gone away, and sometimes it seemed as if we had been born there, as if the earth had given birth to us. From time to time a human figure flitted through the forest, stooping and trembling with fear, and one knew right away: it was a member of one's tribe, being run to earth. One's own fate was no different.

The years of suffering passed, and in 1944 the Red Army liberated us. We wandered across Europe. A sea of homeless people, a strange mixture of doubt and desire for life. Resurrection with no glory. People wandered aimlessly. No one dared to ask "what?" "how?" or "why?" Questions were forbidden. The children's fate was better. The Red Army adopted them as servants in the kitchens and canteens. That was not a particularly brilliant position, but at least they were safe from criminals and perverts for the moment.

The fate of Holocaust survivors is expressed not only in their experiences but also in the answers which they had to give afterwards, to themselves and to others: What happened? How did it happen? Is that really what happened?

The survivor did not know what to do with his experiences. They were more powerful than he, and in any case he saw only ugliness and degeneration in them. If he had been able to keep silent, he would have done so willingly, but something within him, and also his immediate environment, and, if you will, that impulse to seek a moral, did not let him rest. So the matter caught up with him, sometimes in the most irritating manner. "Explain to us, explain," cried the voices from near and far.

What should one tell? Should one tell how when the Second World War broke out one was still a child, an only child, that one's father and mother belonged to the Jewish intelligentsia who believed, in its great innocence, that the world was inclined to progress, and who saw in all nationalism, including Jewish nationalism, merely an anachronism? They were not the only ones whose hearts harbored that desire. Most of the Jewish intelligentsia in Eastern and Central Europe was the same. They denied the existence of evil and refused to see it among others, even when monstrous wickedness was already lurking abroad. But the wickedness was shrewder than they, more cunning than they. It spread its nets everywhere. The awakening, if there was one, came too late. There was nowhere to flee. From then on they were confronted with deportation, separation, murderous shouts in the German language which, just the day before, had been a source of inspiration. Everything came in a furious rush. You had no time to be with yourself. You were already without a mother and father, deprived of everything, thrown out into an alien world without bread.

An error, a misunderstanding, innocence. Perhaps even graver, punishment for self-rejection. Each separate cause by itself, and all of them together. "What happened?" the survivor will ask himself repeatedly over the many years, and sometimes every hour of a single day. A person with an ideological bent will answer accordingly. He will offer explanations or seek a moral. However, most of us are not ideological creatures, and in any case we do not set ourselves up as judges to absolve or condemn.

The reckoning was impossible. Because it was beyond one's power, one took refuge in silence. If you read the many collections of testimony written about the Holocaust, you will immediately see that they are actually repressions, meant to put events in proper chronological order. They are neither introspection nor anything resembling introspection, but rather the careful weaving together of many external facts in order to veil the inner truth. The survivor himself was the first, in the weakness of his own hand and in the denial of his own experiences, to create the strange plural voice of the memoirist, which is nothing but externalization upon externalization, so that what is within will never be revealed.

We quickly fled towards the historical lesson, to seek the lowest common denominator of that horror. There at least is apparently a cause and, seemingly, an effect. A theological moral was immediately added to the historical one. Wise men arose and labored to erect a new theology. But it seems to me that it is not very hard to hear that this is the voice of the intellectual whose faith in God has long been lost, and who finds that now is the proper time to add another justification to the earlier ones.

But let us return to our own memories.

In 1946, on the wave of illegal immigration, we arrived in Palestine: short, skinny, without a language or clothing. Everything that had happened to us during the long years of the war was laid up within us, silent and blind: a mysterious, oppressive mass which had no connection with the consciousness. Of course we knew we were free, but that joy was insufficient to soften the insult of our childhood. Where had we come from and what were we doing here? Sometimes it seemed like a kind of reincarnation whose meaning could not be grasped. The war years had taught us: you are not your own person, will is an illusion. Only blind instinct can show you the way, sometimes. Meanwhile we found ourselves dispersed among farms. After years of wandering and suffering the Land of Israel seemed like a capacious resort, lulling us into deep sleep.

That was, in fact, our wish: to sleep, to sleep for years, to forget ourselves and be reborn. But there was someone who would not allow that desire to sweep us away. He questioned us, and his questions had an evil, metallic, accusatory sound: "What *really* happened there, and how were you saved?"

What could we do with so many memories of death? Live them out? Recount them? Everything seemed too horrible, too unattainable, too far beyond ourselves.

The questions that came from the outside were not helpful. Those questions proceeded from an abyss of misunderstanding, from this world, and they were entirely unconnected with the world from which we came. As if you were to ask for information about hell or about eternity.

So we learned to keep silence. It was not easy to be quiet.

But it was the simplest way out for all of us. Because what is there, in the end, to tell? Even to us everything began to sound fictitious, unbelievable. In that silence of ours there was also the desire to forget, to hide the bitter memories deep in the bottom of the soul, where no stranger's eye, or even our own, can penetrate. That desire was so strong that we managed to do the impossible: neither to speak nor to tell. What didn't we do to conceal that dark secret? We forbade ourselves to reveal anything which might indicate that we had been there. We adopted a handful of Hebrew words to cover and camouflage ourselves. Let no one see the traces of suffering within us. The life instinct, wise and cunning, guided us along that twisted path, and it guided us well. We slowly lost the outward signs of miserable suffering. We became just like the boys from the settlements: tanned, strong, immersed in daily activities. We were no longer asked where we came from and how, and we were pleased that they no longer bothered us with questions.

Of course there were dreams at night, and they tormented us. In that region the horrors retained their full dread, sharp and penetrating, as only a naked dream can be. But the instinct for forgetting, if one may call it that, finally reached that region too, and miraculously, we ceased dreaming as well. A broad living space, in which there were no more restrictions, spread out before us as if we had been born here on these mountaintops, like a local plant.

And in that way the time went by. It seemed as if we had forgotten everything. Our bodies grew stronger, and we flourished in the fresh air. All that had happened to us was conceived, if at all, as a difficult earlier incarnation about which one does not reflect. With the fragrance of the earth we also soaked up our first Hebrew words written in books. The ancient language, which was new to us, was absorbed with clarity within our oblivion. With no regrets we divested ourselves of the few words we had brought from home, the way one takes off an old and worn-out garment.

No days were better than those. Something of the fragrance of childhood returned to us. The fearful spasms of our bodies disappeared, and in their place came elastic movements that no longer feared to touch things.

That was a marvelous oblivion. It nourished us with goodness and gave us only what deep distraction can provide: freedom, lightness, floating. Perhaps that is the way the birds feel between the sky and the earth. At that time we did not know that a certain hostile bitterness was lurking within that marvelous distraction. Perhaps we knew, but we refused to acknowledge its existence.

I have said "forgetfulness," but in fact it was a silent protest against suffering and fate, and more so against the first cause, against our being victims. Everything that had happened to us had only happened because of that fact. Thence the feeling descended to its ugly and painful stage: the victim took the wickedness of the evildoer upon himself. "Something evil lurks within us. It was not for nothing that they persecuted us, not for nothing that they killed us."

The inability to make a reckoning for oneself and the desire to forget joined together in secret and became malice, not the malice of a murderer who commits a crime, but malice directed against ourselves. In the great weakness of his spirit, the victim took the wickedness of the evildoer upon himself, attributing it to himself. Everything that was Jewish, or that seemed Jewish, looked weak, ugly, and damaging to us. What didn't we do in order to root out every link that still bound us to the world from which we had come? We built a kind of private penal colony for ourselves, to expunge every memory so that no sign would be recognizable upon us anymore. In that penal colony no means was unacceptable. On its gate was a single slogan: "Forget. Uproot." Everything was done in the light of that slogan. Yet no one knew of its existence. It was all ours, down to the invisible cells. How long did that violent oblivion continue? Every year changed its colors and every year obscured a different region of life. The moment any memory or shred of a memory was about to float upwards, we would fight against it as though against evil spirits.

The years passed. Life lived on the surface of consciousness continued. It was a dim and dimensionless life based on a kind of fallacy. We knew that something warm and precious within us had been lost on the way to self-forgetfulness, something that we could not deny: parents, scenes from childhood, tribal whispers. Without them, what are we? An ego floating on the surface of consciousness. I said we knew, but we were already in that closed-off territory from which one cannot withdraw.

Our oblivion was so deep that when the day of our awakening came, we were thunderstruck and shocked: we were so far from ourselves that it was as if we had not been born in Jewish homes, and all that had happened to us was nothing but a kind of twilight whose source can no longer be reached. We spoke of the recent past from a strange distance. As if the things had not happened to us.

Oblivion and awakening are the fixed poles between which we have lived for many years. How does one build a bridge across that abyss between the wish to assimilate and the yearning for roots? Do both come from the same source? Will they ever converge? Or is each striving for complete fulfillment on its own, for separation?

Our parents were engaged in a struggle with their tradition, and we were born in its throes. The experiences of the Holocaust distanced us from that controversy. One cannot say that our parents' animosity, revulsion, and long accounting held with their heritage were not transferred to us. On the contrary, we are very familiar with them. Sometimes it seems as if they have found their proper refuge within us. Nevertheless, the experiences of the Holocaust had a kind of gigantic power that drew one into it, into what one's parents had handed on to one, but also what one's grandparents had left one, grandparents who had stood in confusion on the threshold of the modern age, helpless, mocked by their children, who had fled from them towards progress. In other words, the entire structure of Judaism, beliefs and opinions, feelings and emotions, became more dear to one, as if they were one's own. The heart no longer has the power to pick and choose, to say, "This is mine and this not mine," but only to gather up and preserve more and more.

There were years when I believed that the experience of the Holocaust would change us completely, but apparently the shock was too great, the wound too deep, and the tools of our consciousness too meager to bring about such a metamorphosis.

After the war a group of Jews wandered along the open seacoasts of Italy. They refused to live indoors, in sheds, and they earned their bread as migrant laborers in the villages. After the Holocaust, life under a roof seemed not only like a pure absurdity to them but also like the mute acceptance of the illusions inherent in culture, which had brought the darkest demons up from their dark lairs. They chose wandering over the comforts of petit-bourgeois life. Theirs was a form of protest, perhaps also a hint of the kind of life fit for us after the Holocaust. I spent a few months in their company, eating simple food, walking with bare feet, sleeping under the stars, with postponements, sunsets, and silences. I remember these as the dim dawning of some religious experience, which has not departed from me even now.

On that long coast the refugees from the Holocaust split up. Some chose isolation and self-denial, and others chose to attach themselves to every shred and memory of Jewishness. The desire to flee from oneself and one's fate and the wish to cling to every memory were bound together in an uncomfortable combination. And, as after every deluge, there was fear of oneself.

I have not yet spoken about another point which, it seems to me, served as a focus for the feelings which sought unity, and, if you will, relief—and that is the Land of Israel. We children heard about the Land of Israel for the first time in the camps. In the camps there were Bundists, anarchists, communists, and those who had been assimilated for generations. A person does not abandon his faith easily, even in hell. But only about Palestine did people speak in tones that had something in them of faith. During moments of despair, Hebrew songs would burst out from the depths, sounding like songs of religious yearning. Afterwards, in the forests, every once in a while a scrap of sound would reach our ears, torn from a Hebrew song, sounding like the cry of a bird when it feels the dread of a hunter.

That song rose to new life after our liberation. On the long and mournful roads of Europe those Hebrew songs sounded like ancient threnodies.

There were many among us for whom the name "Palestine" rekindled all the fears of the Holocaust: Jews again, once again with clear identifying signs, once again in one place. Many of us fled to distant and far-flung places, to Australia, New Zealand, the Philippines, as far away as possible. Who could have told them not to? There were also others, a few, in whom the name "Palestine" aroused deep longings for roots, for a language, and for faith. You could meet those pilgrims at that time on the bare seacoasts of Italy. While some people were afraid of all contact with Jews and Judaism, fleeing to the ends of the earth, these stood and waited for the ships of the Illegal Immigration, which would come and take them to the Promised Land.

The years, politics, the press, which all have a way of flattening every feeling and belief, also flattened our feeling for the Land of Israel. Every belief is ultimately institutionalized, and the priests learn the routiness. They forget they are priests, and the idea of return to the Land of Israel also has taken on some of the routine qualities of daily life.

In Palestine during those years we sought the meaning of life after death. It was not possible to dress the great wound with a simple bandage. A despoiled youth is a wound that remains open for many years; tortured youth is a wound that will not heal. For some reason, my own destiny propelled me towards literature. In my great naiveté I was certain that it lay within my ability to ask the correct questions. Certainly literature does both ask and answer them in its way, but its strength does not lie in statements, in reproofs, or in preaching, but rather in those details hidden from the eye upon which, if you will, the world stands. The greatness of abstract statements has its place, but literature is obliged, by its own inner laws, to seek out details, and from them, and only from them, to present some truth.

We say the word "Holocaust," and great concepts immediately occur to us: God, destiny, reward and punishment—the essence of metaphysical speculations. But literature, even if it wishes to shout out and shatter the firmament, must first obey a practical imperative: it must deal with the individual, the individual whose father and mother gave him a name, taught him their language, gave him their love, and endowed him with their faith. The dread horrors of the Holocaust challenged the existence of the self, and I do not refer to the biological self which seeks to further its own existence. On the contrary, that self did everything it could, sometimes the impossible, and, if you will, even the inhuman, in order to stay alive. But the self as a spiritual essence, the self as an existing entity with obligations, that self, the essence of the human spirit, was endangered.

In their explicit wickedness, the murderers reduced the Jew to anonymity, a number, a creature with no face. And in fact, years of suffering slowly erased the image of humanity from within the Jew. Only a very few souls, courageous in their faith, were able to retain their humanity in the inferno.

*   *   *

The Holocaust damaged many cells, but the shattering of the self was one of the deepest forms of damage. The feeling of nothingness is not foreign to man, but during the Holocaust that feeling reached proportions that had hitherto been only guessed at.

Who can restore the violated honor of the self? I cannot claim that art is all-powerful, magic, or pure faith, but one virtue cannot be denied it: its loyalty to the individual, its devotion to his suffering and fears, and the bit of light which occasionally sparkles within him.

All true art tirelessly teaches that the whole world rests upon the individual. That is its central point, whether it remains caught up with it or sets forth from it towards society or metaphysical space. The individual, with his own face and proper name, will always be the great subject matter of art.

When people challenge me and ask what is the place of art in that sphere of death and horror, I reply: who can redeem the fears, the pains, the tortures, and the hidden beliefs from the darkness? What will bring them out of obscurity and give them a little warmth and respect, if not art? Who will take that great mass which everyone simply calls the "dreadful horror" and break it up into those tiny, precious particles?

All religious belief is based on two great feelings: the feeling that one is but dust and ashes, and the feeling that man is created in God's image. The equilibrium between these two feelings is what formerly gave the Jew his pride and his humility.

Though one might claim that several of the priestly vessels have been placed in its hands, art cannot replace faith. Art lacks the power for that task, nor does it pretend to possess such power. Nonetheless, by its very nature, art constantly challenges the process by which the individual person is reduced to anonymity. A person is not just a fluid particle caught up in violent historical processes, but a microcosm, which desperately seeks not only its rightful place in the world, but also its own rehabilitation.

LECTURE TWO

First published in *Writing and the Holocaust*, ed. by Berel Lang,
New York and London: Holmes and Meier, 1988.

LECTURE TWO

The subject to be discussed here is horror and art. Can they coexist? Perhaps combining the two is merely another expression of horror, revealing the depths of human degradation. In the concentration camps they forced the prisoners' orchestra to play classical music. For whom were those performances intended, and for what?

The famous saying of Theodor Adorno, that after Auschwitz it would be barbaric to write lyric poetry, is more than understandable. We must agree with it with all our being. A religious person will certainly argue in favor of silence, but what can we do? By his very nature and, if you will, because of his weakness, man has a kind of inner need for ritualization, not only of his joy, but also, and perhaps essentially, of his pain and grief. In the ghettos and the concentration camps, people used to sing a lot, sometimes for hours at a time, in order to banish fear and fortify courage. From the depths I called Thee, God—sometimes those songs were as mighty as the suffering from which they arose.

The need for self-expression in a time of sorrow is ancient and long-standing, and is interwoven throughout the length and breadth of Jewish history. I am repeating that simple fact because one sometimes hears this argument and warning: "Keep literature out of that fire zone. Let the numbers speak, let the documents and the well-established facts speak." I have no wish to belittle that claim, but I do wish to point out that the numbers and the facts were the murderers' own well-proven means. Man as a number is one of the horrors of dehumanization. They never asked anyone who or what he was. They tattooed a number on his arm. Should we seek to tread that path and speak of man in the language of statistics?

In the meantime, however, life has made its own determination. A great deal has already been written about the Holocaust, but if we inquire how much of what has been written is actually literature, we will find that it is quite a small part. When I refer to literature, I do not include all those fantasies about the Holocaust, those commercial productions, perverted stories, and sensational and scandalous writings, which have inundated us since the end of the Second World War. Literature with a true voice and a face one can trust is very scarce. The number of such works could be counted by a child.

What we do have in abundance are memoirs, and we sometimes confuse them with literature. Why has no literature been written—or, if you will, yet been written—about the Holocaust? I shall try to answer that question in a personal way, and of course partially. But before I get to the personal part, I must venture a few words about the quality of the expression that has taken shape so far.

A rich body of testimony has been written about the Holocaust, the testimony of the survivors, and it embodies their whole psychology: haste, inarticulateness, and the lack of all introspection. It is as if what had happened had only happened outside them. The spiritual reckoning, if there is such a thing, was principally concerned with conclusions about society, not with the realm of the soul.

All that was revealed to the Jew during those years was vaster than his reason and his soul. He had been at the very point where the horror took place, and after leaving it he wished to see it as nothing but a nightmare, a rift in life that had to be healed as quickly as possible, a horror that could provide no moral lesson, only a curse.

While the survivor recounts and reveals, at the very same time he also conceals. For it is impossible not to tell, and it is also impossible to admit that what happened did not change him. He remained the same person, bound to the same civil concepts. That revelation and concealment continues to this very day. It seems to me mainly characteristic of the literature of testimony. Such writing must be read with caution, so that one sees not only what is in it, but also, and essentially, what is lacking in it. The survivor's testimony is first of all a search for relief; and as with any burden, the one who bears it seeks also to rid himself of it as hastily as possible. What transpired between him and the dread horrors during his years of suffering? What changed within him, and what will be his way of life from now on? You will not, it seems to me, find answers to these questions. People could not bear witness without encountering obstacles. Agonies of guilt, sometimes alternating with reproaches against the heavens, show up in almost all the testimony, but they are only marginal signs and not the essence of the writing, which is, as I said, in relief.

To avoid misunderstanding, I shall immediately add that the literature of testimony is undoubtedly the authentic literature of the Holocaust. It is an enormous reservoir of Jewish chronology, but it embodies too many inner constraints to become literature as that concept has taken shape over the generations. Those inner constraints are not only psychological.

However, why should I get ahead of myself? Let me return to the descriptive flow, which, more than anything, is personal experience, fragmentary of course, an attempt to trace the development of literary expression, and, if you will, literary nonexpression.

The war revealed to us, to our surprise, that even the most dreadful life of all was nonetheless life. In the ghettos and the camps, people loved, sang sentimental songs, and discussed political party programs. Evening courses in French were given, and peoples drank coffee, if they had any, in the afternoon. On the threshold of death a man still sewed on his buttons. There should be no need to mention that the children played, too. The closer death came to us, the greater was our refusal to admit its existence. Fear faded. Everyone held on to his little hopes—mostly trivial matters, such as taking a bath, for example. As for me, I remember a young man who absolutely refused to be deprived of his mathematics textbooks; he did problems all the time. He did not want to miss out on the second-year course. Those strange mathematics exercises, done between deportation and deportation, made him a tranquil person. In the camps and the ghettos, people played cards a lot, also dominoes and chess. Sometimes, in the good, forgetful moments, it did not seem like a death camp but, rather, like a summer camp for overgrown children deeply engrossed in their play.

For years we lived in the closest proximity to death, but very little thought, if it may be permitted to say so, was devoted to it. The selfish grasping at every crumb of bread and scrap of clothing, that grasping, which was sometimes ugly, was a kind of denial of death. What did people not do to escape it? The world was divided, let us not forget, between black and white in the most unambiguous fashion. That clear division between good and evil gave meaning and purpose to the struggle. And when I say "struggle," I do not refer to any kind of heroics, but to the encouragement one whispered to oneself: Just a little more, it's worth it.

After the war, when the wings of death were folded up, the meaning of life suddenly lost its power and purpose. Sadness, like an iron lid, descended upon the remnants and enclosed them. Reality, which no one could see or wished to see during the war, was now visible in all its starkness: nothing remained except you yourself. That nakedness of yours became a clear writ of accusation. I remember people whose sadness dragged them down with a whisper into a slumber from which they did not rouse again. The wish to sleep was dreadful and tangible. We drank coffee and alcohol in order to stay awake. During the war it seemed that for years, until we reached a ripe old age, we would not cease telling of the horrors of the war. There were people who remained alive only because of the power of that hope: after the war, they would tell. That was, of course, one of the delusions that kept people alive. But beyond that, people felt that they ought to tell about that apocalyptic experience—to interpret it, to analyze it in the tiniest detail, and to examine it from every possible angle.

The struggle for physical survival was harsh and ugly, but that commandment, to remain alive at any price, was, in this case, far more than the commandment to live. It bore within it something of the spirit of a mission. Immediately after the war, that desire was overturned. People were filled with silence. Everything that happened was so gigantic, so inconceivable, that the witness even seemed like a fabricator to himself. The feeling that your experience cannot be told, that no one can understand it, is perhaps one of the worst that was felt by the survivors after the war. Add to that the feeling of guilt, and you find that with your own hands you have built a vast platform of misunderstanding for yourself. The feeling of vocation that throbbed within you in the camps and in the woods became, imperceptibly, an indictment of yourself.

The inability to express your experience and the feeling of guilt combined together and created silence. People have not yet been sufficiently cognizant of that silence. It is true that over the years it has lost some of its strength, it has slipped into the books of testimony. Sometimes it has been fraudulent, but its essence will always remain within that sphere which no expression can encompass.

Not everyone remained within that isolation. The desire to tell, which was latent all those years, broke out and took on strange and different forms of expression. Since new words had not been invented, people made use of the old ones, which had served them before. That was, of course, contemptible and painful.

I would like to take up some of those expressions now. Right after the war, the first entertainment troupes popped up: a mixture of old and young people, among them former actors, singers, youths who had grown up in bunkers, and all sorts of emaciated people who found relief in that distraction. Those troupes were formed spontaneously and went from one transit camp to another; they sang, recited poetry, and told jokes. Were it not for certain grotesque features, they would have been similar to the wandering troupes that used to circulate among the villages to amuse the peasants before the war.

What did those troupes express? It is hard, of course, to generalize. Essentially it was the latent, instinctive desire to live and to restore us to the round of life; on another level it was a kind of protest against suffering and sorrow; but above all, it was forgetfulness. No one knew what to do with the life that had been saved. Sorrow and grief had passed the point of pain and had become something that could no longer be called sorrow and grief.

Since no one knew how to assuage his pain and grief, people sank into shady business deals and smuggling. The latent feeling of guilt created its own destructive means for lowering people to the lowest level of existence. Feverish activity drew people into the depths of oblivion, and at night the entertainment troupes would come and finish the job. Anything, just so as not to be alone with yourself.

At the time, I found these efforts at entertainment disgusting and repugnant. But we ourselves had not yet grasped the depth of the need for them, the innovation, if it may be permitted to say so, in that form. I remember people who protested vehemently against those cheap spectacles and saw them as desecrations. We did not yet understand that we had been deprived of tragedy as well. The regions we inhabited after the war were well beyond the tragic. Tragedy is distinguished by, among other things, conscious knowledge, by the hero's wish to confront his fate directly: tragedy is manifest in the individual, in his well-defined personal suffering. The dimensions of our suffering could not be fully expressed in an individual soul. When the individual attempted merely to become aware of his own consciousness, he collapsed. In the liberated camps, some actors tried to revive the classic Jewish repertory, particularly the tragic plays. Those efforts were, ultimately, more ridiculous than the cheap entertainment troupes. Today, I understand better those inchoate and spontaneous expressions of cheap entertainment. They filled the emptiness that threatened to engulf us. Today, I understand that they were the first harbingers of another form of expression: the comic and grotesque, which then, of course, was still in its infancy.

Alongside light entertainment other forms of expression appeared, of the religious sort, for example. After that enormous catastrophe, the soul seeks a foothold in superstition or, on the contrary, in metaphysics. On the warm coasts of Italy after the war, penitents would wander—rebukers, comforters, preachers, and all sorts of characters within whom metaphysical feelings kindled fiery words. In the great drunken hurly-burly everything seemed like madness. It was the beginning of an inner discussion that evolved and became, over the course of time, the metaphysics of the Holocaust. Light entertainment and religious feelings intermingled after the war, creating a new kind of grotesque. Moral expression was missing. Moral expressions are always of a particular sort, and they arise from norms. The war destroyed, along with the rest, the accepted norms of good and evil. Choice and determination were stolen away completely. It was not who you were, not what you had done, but your being a Jew that was the determining factor in every case. For years we were subject to the blindness of fate. It is no wonder that we came to see the world as a kind of violent caprice. How can you come and say, "Do this" or "Do that," "This is good, that is bad"? Who knows what is good and what is evil? That void left room for a lot of arbitrariness, but also for a great deal of spiritual generosity and self-sacrifice.

Between our quest and our stammerings a great many distortions arose. People published journals that split the suffering down into its minute elements, politicians passed judgment, pseudo-romantic religious writers indulged themselves in reproaches directed against the Supreme Authorities. I do not mean to judge one form of expression or another, but it does seem to be permissible to say that they surrounded the bitter experience with misunderstandings and cheap, simplistic interpretations.

Artistic expression after the Holocaust seems repugnant, disgusting. The pain and suffering called either for silence or for wild outcries. Any embellishment or sweetening was jarring. Moreover, art, and not without reason, was linked in our minds with a sphere of European culture of which we had been the victims.

One evening an old actor from the Vilna troupe appeared in our transit camp. He read the works of the Yiddish poet Raizin. For a moment it seemed as if he was about to lead us back to the past, to what remained of ourselves, but it was precisely that delight which made everyone furious. There was an uproar, and the man left the stage in embarrassment, weeping.

The wish to forget was the strongest of all. It was then that the marvelous instruments of oblivion were created: sleep, bathing in the sea, and, above all, entertainment. Let there be no mention of the war. If it were not for those few who could not repress their experiences, the victims themselves would have denied the horror.

I am purposely mentioning the days right after the war. Then there arose, inchoate and inarticulate, the first efforts at expression. That which came later was only an expansion on those beginnings, or their impoverishment. The desire to keep silence and the desire to speak became deeper; and only artistic expression, which came years later, could attempt to bridge those two difficult imperatives. Artistic expression did not arise quickly. It called for a human form that would hint at the available possibilities.

The new "form," if one may call it that, was discovered by the children. They were survivors, and the war years in forests and monasteries had molded their faces and expression. Some of them sang well. I say well, even though their voices were generally cracked. Their songs were the remnants of melodies from their Jewish homes and scraps from the monastery organs. It all came together in them in a new kind of melody that only children, in their blindness, could create. You could call it innocent or just inelegant. They stood up on crates and sang. At the end of their performance, they would pass around their tattered hats and ask for payment. Violent managers quickly took them under their protection, and they would drag them from camp to camp. There were also girls. I remember one of them well. Her name was Amalia. She was about ten, and she would perform every night. Her repertory was a mixture of Yiddish songs and forest noises. Her thin, birdlike body always seemed as if it were about to fly away.

There were child acrobats who walked tightropes with marvelous skill. In the woods they had learned how to climb in the highest, thinnest branches. Among them was a set of twins, boys of about ten, who juggled wooden balls fantastically. There were also child mimics who would imitate animals and birds. Dozens of children like that wandered around the camps. While the adults tried to forget what had happened and to forget themselves, to get back into the fabric of life, the children refined their suffering as, perhaps, can be done only in a folk song.

I have discussed the children because it was from them, in the course of time, that artistic expression arose. I shall try to explain myself. Ultimately the children did not absorb the full horror, only that portion of it which children could take in. Children lack a sense of chronology, of comparison with the past. While the adults spoke about what had been, for the children the Holocaust was the present, their childhood and youth. They knew no other childhood. Or happiness. They grew up in dread. They knew no other life.

While the adults fled from themselves and from their memories, repressing them and building up a new life in place of their previous one, the children had no previous life or, if they had, it was now effaced. The Holocaust was the black milk, as the poet said, that they sucked morning, noon, and night.

That psychological aspect also had ideological significance. The Holocaust is sometimes conceived, even among its victims, as an episode, as madness, as an eclipse that does not belong to the normal flow of time, a volcanic eruption of which one must beware, but which indicates nothing about the rest of life.

The Holocaust as life, as life in its most dreadfully concentrated form from both the existential and social point of view—that approach was rejected by the victim. The numerous books of testimony that were written about the Holocaust are, if you will, a desperate effort to force the Holocaust into a remote recess of madness, to cut it off from life, and in other cases, to envelop it in a kind of mystical aura, intangible, which must be discussed as a kind of experience that cannot be expressed in words, but rather in prolonged silence. In the case of the children who grew up in the Holocaust, life during the Holocaust was something they could understand, for they had absorbed it in their blood. They knew man as a beast of prey, not metaphorically, but as a physical reality with his full stature and clothing, his way of standing and sitting, his way of caressing his own child and of beating a Jewish child.

We would sit for hours and observe. Hunger, thirst, and

weakness made us observant creatures. Rather than the murderers, we observed their victims, in their weakness and in their heroism. Those tortured faces on the brink of the chasm will not be forgotten. To "be forgotten" is not the correct expression. They were stamped upon us the way childhood is stamped upon the matrix of one's flesh.

Most of us had no words, and it is therefore no wonder that our first artistic expressions were drawings. The children made a lot of drawings, even in the death camps. The poems and drawings created by the children in Theresienstadt bear witness to that power, which in its refinement is close to the folk song and naive art.

Artistic consciousness came later. There was a need not only for perspective, but also for some new orientation. Orientation after the Holocaust meant oblivion, flight from oneself and from one's Jewishness. Only a few of the Holocaust survivors reached Israel. Most of them preferred to be scattered throughout the world, to distant and remote places. The land of Israel was considered, and not incorrectly, to be Judaism, itself a danger that must be fled.

The children, of course, had no choice. No one wanted orphans. The ships of the Illegal Immigration accepted people indiscriminately—children, old people, and the sick.

It is strange to say so, but one must say so. There was a need for some kind of unmediated relation, simple and straightforward, to those horrible events in order to speak about them in artistic terms. Neither sublimation nor apologetics, and not glorification, but rather the way a person speaks about the events of his life, as terrible as they may be, but still and all, life. That way of speaking was the children's lot. That is how they expressed themselves when they were in the concentration camps, and afterward in the liberated camps; and something of that unmediated quality remained with them even after they grew up and sought themselves as human beings and as Jews.

Over the years the problem, and not only the artistic problem, has been to remove the Holocaust from its enormous, inhuman dimensions and bring it close to human beings. Without that effort it would remain a distant and unseen nightmare, somewhere off in the distance of time, where it would be easy to forget. It is the great Jewish experience, also a non-Jewish experience, and if it is not assimilated as it ought to be, one day we will be like grown-up children who have been deprived of a basic truth of life.

By its nature, when it comes to describing reality, art always demands a certain intensification, for many and various reasons. However, that is not the case with the Holocaust. Everything in it already seems so thoroughly unreal, as if it no longer belongs to the experience of our generation, but to mythology. Thence comes the need to bring it down to the human realm. That is not a mechanical problem, but an essential one. When I say "to bring it down," I do not mean to simplify, to attenuate, or to sweeten the horror, but to attempt to make the events speak through the individual and in his language, to rescue the suffering from huge numbers, from dreadful anonymity, and to restore the person's given and family name, to give the tortured person back his human form, which was snatched away from him.

There is a tendency to speak of the Holocaust in mystical terms, to link the events to the incomprehensible, the mysterious, the insane, and the meaningless. That tendency is both understandable and dangerous, from every point of view. Murder that was committed with evil intentions must not be interpreted in mystical terms. A vile hand was raised against mankind: we do not have mysticism here, but a blow directed against the central pillar of the Ten Commandments.

LECTURE THREE

LECTURE THREE

The fate of the people who survived the Holocaust is embodied not only in their experience but also in the answers which they had to supply afterwards, both to themselves and to others. The questions they faced were not easy ones, and in many cases the survivor stood as if accused. He was accused of blindness, of impotence, and of cowardice. The phrase "Led like sheep to the slaughter" summarizes, it seems to me, all of those accusations.

The accusers knew that not all the Jewish men were of fighting age. "Do not abandon your father and mother" is one of the basic commandments of Judaism. The accusers also knew that all of Europe was united in one joint purpose, to destroy the Jews. These facts were known, but nevertheless they did not seem to be taken into account. Many people thought that it was shameful that millions of Jews were led to the slaughter without resistance, shameful and difficult to accept or bear.

Hence we have that complex relationship, full of suspicion and misunderstanding, between the survivor and those about him. Like all misunderstandings and suspicions, these also produced inner constraints and complexes, an intricate structure of rationalizations which kept the truth at a distance on all sides.

When the people around them spoke of sheep led to the slaughter, the survivors spoke of the Warsaw Ghetto and the partisans. That relationship of accusation and self-defense was prolonged for quite a few years in Israel. Enormous catastrophes are often perceived as bitter failures, and they bring into being, consciously or unconsciously, accused and accusers.

I am saying these things by way of introduction, because the topic of our discussion today, the Holocaust and religious faith, is also subject to misunderstanding. I shall begin by considering the assumption commonly accepted by many people, that the Holocaust weakened the religious faith of many of its victims, if it did not destroy that faith. I do not know when or where that rumor originated, but it is so widely current that it has become a truism which is never challenged.

Deep faith is not something easily thrown off. Anyone who lived through the Holocaust will never forget the cries of "Hear O Israel" which shattered the air and shook the earth. The lives of the Jews were wrenched away not only in fear, but sometimes also in spiritual exaltation and true martyrdom.

During the Holocaust, and one must not deny it, ugly scenes were played out between people and their families, between man and his fellowman, as in every catastrophe. There were also traitors, talebearers, and thieves. The fear of death is a dreadful fear. It can bring a man to commit the ugliest of deeds. "Do not lead us into temptation," says the ancient prayer. Our sages knew what they were talking about.

Dreadful sights, the abandonment of parents, the betrayal

of children and friends, are not strange to anyone who lived through the Holocaust. People faced trials far beyond human capacity. The choice was horrible, mostly inhuman. Nevertheless, the will to live was not the only active force. During every Nazi "Aktion" countless deeds of Jewish heroism took place. It must be known that every survivor survived not only through his own efforts, but principally because of the generous and heroic deeds of his fellows.

The horrors of the Holocaust did not last only a day or two. They lasted for six years. I doubt whether there are six years as long as those in all of Jewish history. They were years during which every minute, second, and fraction of a second was filled beyond its capacity. There was no feeling or thought which was not refined in the furnace of suffering. We speak of the Holocaust as if it were just physical suffering. But there was no less spiritual suffering. While dread assailed you from without, feverish spiritual sufferings raged within you. Who is man? Who is a Jew? In the penal colony those torments were our bread and water.

The Holocaust did not catch the Jew with his ancient faith at its most powerful, but at a moment of weakness, when he was trying to find his way. Considerable portions of the Jewish people had already passed beyond the bounds of their Jewishness. The woods and the bunkers not only provided shelter against the enemy, but also served as a kind of retreat allowing one to get to the source of all that suffering. In the woods and the bunkers vehement discussions would last until dawn. The Jew faced not only the Nazis, but also his own Jewishness, which was haunting him. The inner blaze was no less intense than the fire from the outside.

I hesitate to say it, but one must: The apocalyptic horror of the Holocaust was felt by us as a deeply religious experience. It is not easy to say that, because it is sometimes hard

45

to explain it, even to oneself. When I say that it was a religious experience, I do not refer to the abstract area of theology, but primarily to experiences in man's relations to his fellowman and in his relations to the material world around him. The quality of the bond and relationship which was created between one and one's surroundings, between one and oneself, was a new one. Those subtle and searing experiences are not easily expressed or defined, and I doubt whether it is possible to present them as evidence, though it seems that they were clear sparks of light in the absolute darkness, moments of release from one's physical being, and of Jewish brotherhood beyond tribal unity.

During the Holocaust we saw clearly how observant Jews raised the commandments to a level of absolute purity. We saw how religious practices such as observing kashrut and the sabbath and praying at the correct time became not only the pillars of religion but also columns of fire that illuminated the darkness of those who had never before known the commandments of Judaism in their lives.

Most of my generation had been strangers to the secrets of the Jewish religion. Our Judaism, if we had any, was social, rationalistic. Rather than a life of experience, it was a matter of routine, and here, in the thick of the horror, the encounter with our Jewishness took place, not by reason or by apologetics, but, as it were, an unmediated encounter. Jewish history in its most concentrated form stood before us, face to face.

The horror stripped us, in a single stroke, of all our garments. A great community of Jews, perhaps the greatest in Jewish history, stood with no shelter, deprived of all their earthly possessions, deprived of every title and position. Only the individual himself stood in that arena, defenseless, without any choice, apology, justification, or plea for

46

mercy. The great and small stood as equals, and the whole world was embodied in the figure of the hangman. The transports, the ghettos, and the camps—never was such a cruel reality created. Nevertheless, everything also seemed to be taking place in another sphere as well, in some dread spiritual realm.

The Jew was dragged from trial to trial, and his only guilt was the Jewish mystery within him. "What is there within me that makes me the enemy of mankind? Perhaps it is my build, the way I think. And what is the nature of those judges? They are cultured people, graduates of gymnasia, physicians, attorneys, and judges. Where did they get their immense power to torment women and children?"

Humane reason, which the Jew cultivated with great faith and devotion, and sometimes even at the expense of his own Jewish values, that humane reason became, before his very eyes, a demon. In the penal colony a man was not measured by what he was, but by that mystery which he, as it were, bore within him. It did not matter whether he accepted that mystery as something real and an inseparable part of his existence, or whether he alienated himself from it. "Against your will you are born," said our sages, "against your will you live, against your will you die." The Holocaust added: "Against your will you are a Jew."

The naive faith that a man was free, to be judged by his intentions and acts, everything that we include under the rubric of "humane rationalism," crumbled and turned to dust. In the penal colony other standards were set. The mystery within you was crime and punishment at one and the same time. As I said, not a few of us revolted against that fate, even at the edge of the abyss. But for others, also not a few, it was a point of light, a voiceless return to the source of which they had been deprived.

That process, which took place deep within the soul, cannot be encompassed with words. I hesitate to use concepts from our ancient tradition. Lately in Israel the term "hazara biteshuva," translated as "repentance," literally meaning a "return" to religious observance, has taken on a social, if not a political, dimension that endangers its ancient and deep meaning, and that is why I am wary of using it. Moreover, that "repentance" is generally taken to mean a total return, the complete acknowledgment and acceptance of divine authority. What happened during the Holocaust was not that sort of "return," but rather contact with an atmosphere permeated by a kind of mythic depth, the stratum out of which, it seems to me, faith arises. It is also possible, of course, to say that the religious feeling emerged in the height of despair and at an equal distance from nihilism. If a religious feeling arose, it was not because of some kind of fatalism which a person imposes upon himself as the ultimate alternative of life. It was a kind of "in spite of everything," essentially human, a sense of obligation to Jewish suffering and pain. That obligation can be seen in different ways, starting from the simplest emotional reaction—revulsion at the beast within man—and culminating in a commitment that stated: If fate has decreed that we must be Jews, then let us be Jews.

Religious feelings during the Holocaust broke out on all sides, expressed silently, and in the sounds of song and prayer. I have already spoken about the collective religious feeling, about the togetherness, about our being bereft of all property, social status, and title, about the way we confronted existence face to face and stood before the murderers—but it seems to me that religious feelings, or what I am calling religious feelings, were especially intense in each of our hearts, by ourselves.

48

Here I ought, perhaps, to say a word about the qualities of the religious feelings to which I refer. Mostly they were "illuminations" after days of hunger, danger, and despair, a sense of wonder about people or objects, a kind of contact with one's parents, self-consolation.

For the children it was perhaps more "primordial"— contact with the trees in the forest, the moist earth, the straw, sucking fluids from the roots of the trees, the night skies. Those contacts with a hostile space, for us, homeless and orphaned, had a quality that was beyond "discovery" or curiosity.

I call those feelings religious, the fundamental religious sentiments, if you will, since they do not raise questions and they are not angry rebukes, nor are they far-reaching searchings of the soul, but rather wonder for its own sake, without any ulterior intention: you and the world, with no separation. Those feelings arose and persisted during moments of relative calm, between deportation and deportation, or sometimes in the forests during the mild seasons. Those feelings were few, but they were so powerful that they were able to nourish us during the days of cold and suffering with a marvelous measure of consolation. I can imagine that one might object to calling such feelings religious. People with a traditional religious outlook would call them fetishism. Moreover, I have encountered a fair number of people who lived through the Holocaust and who never were visited by feelings such as those. They do not understand what we are talking about. If I may speak from my own experience, I remember sitting beside a pond in the forest, looking at twigs floating on its surface, observing them with a kind of "devotion," as if they were not twigs but rather enchanted objects which had come to me from a great distance.

The wandering, dangers, and longings for our parents turned us not only into hunted animals who had lost every vestige of humanity, but also into creatures of yearning. Out of my great longing for my parents, I transported them to my hiding place, and I used to speak with them as if they were sitting by my side. Those conversations gave me a kind of joy and confidence, but above all, a feeling that I was not alone in the world. After the war other children told me that they too had feelings like that in the forests.

Many years afterwards I noticed that a close friend of mine, with whom I went through some times during the war, frequently uses the word "shame," even when he is speaking of a small error on his part, or an insignificant mistake, not a failure of any kind. His habit indicates a kind of exaggerated self-accusation. Another friend, a very practical person, who is now in his sixties, reacts differently to his own errors: he covers his eyes with his right hand, a way of concentrating, apparently.

The Holocaust has become an issue. It has been grafted onto the study of history, become a theological concern and a chapter of Jewish literature. For the survivors of the Holocaust, it is still an experience that seeks its redemption. Clearly time has healed some wounds, the details have softened slightly, but occasionally spasms rise from the depths of the past and show that the circle has not been completely closed, that the debt is still haunting the debtor.

I wish to say a few words about the nature of that incompleteness. Most Holocaust survivors are burdened with a feeling of guilt. Since that feeling is not clear, since it is undefined, it has assumed various guises over the years. Along with the guilt feeling, in parallel with it, if you will, there is also a desire for atonement. If the guilt were clear, the expressions of atonement could also be formulated with a certain clarity. But since the feeling of guilt has remained in a deep hollow of mystery, the expressions of atonement have also failed to find a clear outlet.

I knew many people who, after the Holocaust, no longer saw any reason to live a normal life, and they became recluses. I use the word "recluse" intentionally, because it refers to an essentially voluntary act, with religious overtones. It took much courage to return to a normal way of life. Seclusion, which certainly entails a kind of withdrawal and revulsion, was more fitting for us than the noisy round of life. But the recluses were in the minority, I believe.

In fact, what is characteristic of Holocaust survivors was not seclusion but rather activity, sometimes excessive activity bound up with a powerful ambition not just to become active, but to make other people act. In the liberated camps that activism was already frenetic, and it became stronger over the years. Among Holocaust survivors you find highly practical people whose activity has brought them prominence and earned them great wealth.

"To live, to live at any price." That cry, whose source is in Jewish optimism, which knows no limits, has done its work. Anyone who saw the remnants absorbed in the kibbutzim, the villages, and the cities of Israel during the late forties had a foretaste of the resurrection of the dead. However, neither seclusion nor activism were guided by a conscious sense of purpose. They were, more than anything, a reaction: two ways of grasping life, two ways of fighting against chaos and madness. I do not mean to claim that the seclusion bore nothing of religious meditation, or that the feverish activism had nothing to do with the ancient Jewish commandments. They did, but only a hint. In no way did they have full religious significance.

The Jewish religion has, of course, long experience with catastrophe, but it was unable to absorb and assimilate such a mass of pain. The simple-minded explanation of reward and punishment which rabbis and theologians offered so effortlessly was an insult to honest feeling.

Therefore, even though many years have passed, perhaps because so many years have passed, the demand for meaning becomes increasingly pressing. While previously the hidden and unarticulated accusation dogged us, now we hear a different demand: for meaning!

Most of us have to live with the feeling that we have done only the tiniest little bit of what was demanded from us. Normal life, insofar as we took to it, not only failed to moderate our distress, sometimes it also made our anguish burn hotter. As the years passed, the feeling grew stronger that what had been entrusted to us had slipped away, and not only through inactivity. On the contrary, if you will, there was a great deal of activity: monuments were erected, volumes of testimony were compiled, and research has flourished. Hardly a month passes without some kind of congress or symposium about the Holocaust. All that activity is directed outward. But within oneself, one knows that, with one's own manner of thinking and feeling, one has not managed to turn the experience of the Holocaust into a spiritual element in life. By tirelessly repeating, "It's too vast for my understanding," we have relegated our experience to the pigeonhole that has been set aside for it: "infinite suffering which has no meaning." Since that is the case, survivors have clung to normal life as an honorable way out.

The clinging to normality, which is rightly considered to be a real personal achievement and contribution to stability—good citizenship, in short, respectable petit-bourgeois activity—did not bring with it what it was intended to bring. For that accomplishment, which up to a few years ago had been a source of pride, has not passed the test of time. To be a decent citizen after the experience of Auschwitz is doubtless a considerable personal achievement and a social contribution, but it cannot be interpreted as a spiritual victory.

It is no coincidence that the desire to give metaphysical meaning to the Holocaust arose quite late. I know several people who surprisingly took up religious belief in its traditional, institutional form. However, with most of us, the roots of institutional faith were damaged beyond repair, even among those of us who recognized that faith is ultimately an institution as well. We just could not force our experience into narrow confines. Thus we found ourselves with a double loss.

With a bit of national enthusiasm, but without institutional religious faith, we were drawn, like everyone else, into the great camp of the petite bourgeoisie, which began to take shape in Israel during the fifties and sixties, and this is what it offered us: activity, personal profit, competition, careers of every sort, and, above all, profound self-forgetfulness. It is definitely possible to say that the Holocaust survivors made a place for themselves in the society. You find them in every suburb and office. They manage factories, they own luxurious apartments, and some of them teach in the universities. In the hidden recesses of their hearts they hoped that their children would share something of their experience. That was very important to them, but in reality they strained, for many understandable reasons, to hide the past and sometimes to lie about it in order not to disrupt the full happiness of their offspring. Why tell them? Why darken their lives? What good will it do?

Just a few years passed. They soon realized that their offspring had absorbed rumors and information from the out-side, pale ciphers without any real relation to the experience which had molded their parents. Now it was too late. It is difficult to make amends for what one has not done in time. How should one make amends? One should explain everything from the start. But who could understand it?

Their petit-bourgeois life is a burden to them, but it is already part of them. The years have made of them what their experiences did not do: people of settled minds. The price was high, and still they are not reconciled. Sometimes you see a friend's face, and it is veiled in shame.

Today it seems that no one says, "I don't understand," or "It's too enormous for me." With the passing years, the bywords have become expressions of surprise: How did we manage? How were we changed from creatures who lived for years in close proximity to death, to become a kind of petit-bourgeois spirit, surrounded by the comforts of home, without any vision, and deeply immersed in routine?

That great experience, because it was never assimilated, sometimes transformed those who had undergone it into caricatures. You can see those caricatures in various places: at academic conferences, symposia, memorials, banquets. I remember one memorial ceremony attended by former prisoners of Auschwitz. The men wore fine suits, the women were adorned with gold. The tables were laden with fine food, and between the courses people told of their experiences, gave speeches, distributed grants, and spoke about their coming vacations in Israel. If you wish, that is a kind of life, life for which one should be grateful, but, if you will, it is plainly also a stark caricature of life.

There is no doubt that the war dulled, distorted, and, I do not hesitate to say so, corrupted the soul, but at the same time it also brought out powers of dedication and self-sacrifice from the depths, and mainly archaic feelings that, over the years, had been covered beneath a thick deposit of rationalism.

We are used to thinking that the Second World War extinguished the last spark of Jewish faith. That is not the case. Like every volcanic eruption, the Holocaust brought up strata from the depths. The question remains, however, and will always remain: How can we transform it into a spiritual vision?

A CONVERSATION WITH
PHILIP ROTH

First published in *The New York Times Book Review*, 28 February 1988; *London Review of Books*, 17 March 1988.

A CONVERSATION
WITH
PHILIP ROTH

Aharon Appelfeld lives a few miles west of
Jerusalem in a maze-like conglomeration of attractive
stone dwellings directly next to an "absorption center,"
where immigrants are temporarily housed, schooled, and
prepared for life in their new society. The arduous journey
that landed Appelfeld on the beaches of Tel Aviv in 1946,
at the age of fourteen, seems to have fostered an unap-
peasable fascination with all uprooted souls, and at the local
grocery where he and the absorption center residents do
their shopping, he will often initiate an impromptu conversation with an Ethiopian, or a Russian, or a Rumanian Jew
still dressed for the climate of a country to which he or she
will never return.

The living room of the two-story apartment is simply
furnished: some comfortable chairs, books in three languages on the shelves, and on the walls impressive adoles-
cent drawings by the Appelfelds' son Meir, who is now
twenty-one and, since finishing his military duty, has been
studying art in London. Yitzak, eighteen, recently com-
pleted high school and is in the first of his three years of
compulsory Army service. Still at home is twelve-year-old
Batya, a clever girl with the dark hair and blue eyes of her

Argentinian Jewish mother, Appelfeld's youthful, good-natured wife, Judith. The Appelfelds appear to have created as calm and harmonious a household as any child could hope to grow up in. During the four years that Aharon and I have been friends, I don't think I've ever visited him at home in Mevasseret Zion without remembering that his own childhood—as an escapee from a Nazi work camp, on his own in the primitive wilds of the Ukraine—provides the grimmest possible antithesis to this domestic ideal.

A portrait photograph that I've seen of Aharon Appelfeld, an antique-looking picture taken in Czernowicz, Bukovina, in 1938, when Aharon was six, and brought to Palestine by surviving relatives, shows a delicately refined bourgeois child seated alertly on a hobbyhorse and wearing a beautiful sailor suit. You simply cannot imagine this child, only twenty-four months on, confronting the exigencies of surviving for years as a hunted and parentless little boy in the woods. The keen intelligence is certainly there, but where is the robust cunning, the animalish instinct, the biological tenacity that it took to endure that terrifying adventure?

As much is secreted away in that child as in the writer he's become. At fifty-five, Aharon is a small, bespectacled, compact man with a perfectly round face and a perfectly bald head and the playfully thoughtful air of a benign wizard. He'd have no trouble passing for a magician who entertains children at birthday parties by pulling doves out of a hat—it's easier to associate his gently affable and kindly appearance with that job than with the responsibility by which he seems inescapably propelled: responding, in a string of elusively portentous stories, to the disappearance from Europe—while he was outwitting peasants and foraging in the forests—of just about all the continent's Jews, his parents among them.

His literary subject is not the Holocaust, however, or even Jewish persecution. Nor, to my mind, is what he writes simply Jewish fiction or, for that matter, Israeli fiction. Nor, since he is a Jewish citizen of a Jewish state composed largely of immigrants, is his an exile's fiction. And, despite the European locale of many of his novels and the echoes of Kafka, these books written in the Hebrew language certainly aren't European fiction. Indeed, all that Appelfeld is not adds up to what he is, and that is a dislocated writer, a deported writer, a dispossessed and uprooted writer, Appelfeld is a displaced writer of displaced fiction, who has made of displacement and disorientation a subject uniquely his own. His sensibility—marked almost at birth by the solitary wanderings of a little bourgeois boy through an ominous nowhere—appears to have spontaneously generated a style of sparing specificity, of out-of-time progression and thwarted narrative drives, that is an uncanny prose realization of the displaced mentality. As unique as the subject is a voice that originates in a wounded consciousness pitched somewhere between amnesia and memory, and that situates the fiction it narrates midway between parable and history.

Since we met in 1984, Aharon and I have talked together at great length, usually while walking through the streets of London, New York, and Jerusalem. I've known him over these years as an oracular anecdotalist and folkloristic enchanter, as a wittily laconic kibbitzer and an obsessive dissector of Jewish states of mind—of Jewish aversions, delusions, remembrances, and manias. However, as is often the case in friendships between writers, during these peripatetic conversations we had never really touched on each other's work—that is, not until last month, when I traveled to Jerusalem to discuss with him the six of his fifteen published books that are now in English translation.

After our first afternoon together we disencumbered ourselves of an interloping tape recorder and, though I took some notes along the way, mostly we talked as we've become accustomed to talking—wandering down city streets or sitting in coffee shops where we'd stop to rest. When finally there seemed to be little left to say, we sat down together and tried to synthesize on paper—I in English, Aharon in Hebrew—the heart of the discussion. Aharon's answers to my questions have been translated by Jeffrey Green.

PR: I find echoes in your fiction of two Middle European writers of a previous generation: Bruno Schulz, the Polish Jew who wrote in Polish and was shot and killed at fifty by the Nazis in Drogobycz, the heavily Jewish Galician city where he taught high school and lived at home with his family, and Kafka, the Prague Jew who wrote in German and also lived, according to Max Brod, "spellbound in the family circle" for most of his forty-one years. You were born 500 miles east of Prague, 125 miles southeast of Drogobycz, in Czernowicz. Your family—prosperous, highly assimilated, German-speaking—bore certain cultural and social similarities to Kafka's, and, like Schulz, you, along with your family, suffered personally the Nazi horror. The affinity that interests me, however, isn't biographical but literary and, though I see signs of it throughout your work, it's particularly clear in *The Age of Wonders*. The opening scene, for instance, depicting a mother and her adoring twelve-year-old luxuriating on a train journey home from their idyllic summer vacation, reminds me of similar scenes in Schulz stories. And only a few pages on there is a Kafka-esque surprise when the train stops unexpectedly by a dark old sawmill and the security forces request that all Austrian passengers who are not Christians by birth register at the sawmill's office. I'm reminded of *The Trial*—of *The Castle*, as well—where there is at the outset an ambiguously menacing assault on the legal status of the hero. Tell me, how pertinent to your imagination do you consider Kafka and Schulz to be?

AA: I discovered Kafka here in Israel during the 1950s, and as a writer he was close to me from my first contact. He spoke to me in my mother tongue, German, not the German of the Germans but the German of the Hapsburg Empire, of Vienna, Prague, and Czernowicz, with its special tone, which, by the way, the Jews worked hard to create.

To my surprise he spoke to me not only in my mother tongue, but also in another language which I knew intimately, the language of the absurd. I knew what he was talking about. It wasn't a secret language for me and I didn't need any explications. I had come from the camps and the forests, from a world that embodied the absurd, and nothing in that world was foreign to me. What was surprising was this: How could a man who had never been there know so much, in precise detail, about that world?

Other surprising discoveries followed: the marvel of his objective style, his preference for action over interpretation, his clarity and precision, the broad, comprehensive view laden with humor and irony. And, as if that weren't enough, another discovery showed me that behind the mask of placelessness and homelessness in his work stood a Jewish man, like me, from a half-assimilated family, whose Jewish values had lost their content, and whose inner space was barren and haunted.

The marvelous thing is that the barrenness brought him not to self-denial or self-hatred but rather to a kind of tense curiosity about every Jewish phenomenon, especially the Jews of Eastern Europe, the Yiddish language, the Yiddish theatre, Hasidism, Zionism, and even the idea of moving to Mandate Palestine. This is the Kafka of his journals, which are no less gripping than his works. I found a palpable embodiment of Kafka's Jewish involvement in his Hebrew handwriting, for he had studied Hebrew and knew it. His handwriting is clear and amazingly beautiful, showing his effort and concentration as in his German handwriting, but his Hebrew handwriting has an additional aura of love for the isolated letter.

Kafka revealed to me not only the plan of the absurd world but also the charms of its art, which I needed as an assimilated Jew. The fifties were years of search for me, and Kafka's works illuminated the narrow path which I tried to blaze for myself. Kafka emerges from an inner world and tries to get some grip on reality, and I came from a world of detailed empirical reality, the camps and the forests. My real world was far beyond the power of imagination, and my task as an artist was not to develop my imagination but to restrain it, and even then it seemed impossible to me, because everything was so unbelievable that one seemed oneself to be fictional.

At first I tried to run away from myself and from my memories, to live a life that was not my own and to write about a life that was not my own. But a hidden feeling told me that I was not allowed to flee from myself, and that if I denied the experience of my childhood in the Holocaust, I would be spiritually deformed. Only when I reached the age of thirty did I feel the freedom to deal as an artist with those experiences.

To my regret, I came to Bruno Schulz's work years too late, after my literary approach was rather well formed. I felt and still feel a great affinity with his writing, but not the same affinity I feel with Kafka.

PR: Of your six books translated now into English, *The Age of Wonders* is the one in which an identifiable historical background is most sharply delineated. The narrator's writer-father is an admirer of Kafka's; in addition, the father is party, we are told, to an intellectual debate about Martin Buber; we're also told that he's a friend of Stefan Zweig's. But this specificity, even if it doesn't develop much beyond these few references to an outside world, is not common in the books of yours I've read. Hardship generally fells your Jews the way the overpowering ordeal descends, in Kafka, on his victims: inexplicably, out of nowhere, in a society seemingly without history or politics. "What do they want of us?" asks a Jew in *Badenheim 1939*, after he's gone to register as a Jew at, of all places, the Badenheim Sanitation Department. "It's hard to understand," another Jew answers.

There's no news from the public realm that might serve as a warning to an Appelfeld victim, nor is the victim's impending doom presented as part of a European catastrophe. The historical focus is supplied by the reader, who understands, as the victims cannot, the magnitude of the enveloping evil. Your reticence as a historian, when combined with the historical perspective of a knowing reader, accounts for the peculiar impact your work has—for the power that emanates from stories that are told through such very modest means. Also, dehistoricizing the events and blurring the background, you probably approximate the disorientation felt by people who were unaware that they were on the brink of a cataclysm.

It's occurred to me that the perspective of the adults in your fiction resembles in its limitations the viewpoint of a child, who, of course, has no historical calendar in which to place unfolding events and no intellectual means of penetrating their meaning. I wonder if your own consciousness as a child at the edge of the Holocaust isn't mirrored in the simplicity with which the imminent horror is perceived in your novels.

AA: Your're right. In *Badenheim 1939* I completely ignored the historical explanation. I assumed that the historical facts were known to readers and that they would fill in what was missing. You're also correct, it seems to me, in assuming that my description of the Second World War has something in it of a child's vision, but I'm not sure whether the ahistorical quality of *Badenheim 1939* derives from the child's vision that's preserved within me. Historical explanations have been alien to me every since I became aware of myself as an artist. And the Jewish experience in the Second World War was not "historical." We came into contact with archaic mythical forces, a kind of dark subconscious the meaning of which we did not know, nor do we know it to this day. This world appears to be rational (with trains, departure times, stations, and engineers), but in fact these were journeys of the imagination, lies and ruses, which only deep, irrational drives could have invented. I didn't understand, nor do I yet understand, the motives of the murderers.

I was a victim, and I try to understand the victim. That is a broad, complicated expanse of life that I've been trying to deal with for thirty years now. I haven't idealized the victims. I don't think that in *Badenheim 1939* there's any idealization either. By the way, Badenheim is a rather real place, and spas like that were scattered all over Europe, shockingly petit bourgeois and idiotic in their formalities. Even as a child I saw how ridiculous they were.

It is generally agreed, to this day, that Jews are deft, cunning, and sophisticated creatures, with the wisdom of the world stored up in them. But isn't it fascinating to see how easy it was to fool the Jews? With the simplest, almost childish tricks they were gathered up in ghettos, starved for months, encouraged with false hopes, and finally sent to their death by train. That ingenuousness stood before my eyes while I was writing *Badenheim*. In that ingenuousness I found a kind of distillation of humanity. Their blindness and deafness, their obsessive preoccupation with themselves, is an integral part of their ingenuousness. The murderers were practical, and they knew just what they wanted. The ingenuous person is always a shlemazl, a clownish victim of misfortune, never hearing the danger signals in time, getting mixed up, tangled up, and finally falling in the trap. Those weaknesses charmed me. I fell in love with them. The myth that the Jews run the world with their machinations turned out to be somewhat exaggerated.

PR: Of all your translated books, *Tzili* depicts the harshest reality and the most extreme form of suffering. Tzili, the simplest child of a poor Jewish family, is left alone when her family flees the Nazi invasion. The novel recounts her horrendous adventures in surviving and her excruciating loneliness among the brutal peasants for whom she works. The books strikes me as a counterpart to Jerzy Kosinski's *Painted Bird*. Though less grotesque, *Tzili* portrays a fearful child in a world even bleaker and more barren that Kosinski's, a child moving in isolation through a landscape as uncongenial to human life as any in Beckett's *Molloy*.

As a boy you wandered alone like Tzili after your escape, at eight, from the camp. I've been wondering why, when you came to transform your own life in an unknown place, hiding out among the hostile peasants, you decided to imagine a girl as the survivor of this ordeal. And did it occur to you ever not to fictionalize this material but to present your experiences as you remember them, to write a survivor's tale as direct, say, as Primo Levi's depiction of his Auschwitz incarceration?

AA: I have never written about things as they happened. All my works are indeed chapters from my most personal experience, but nevertheless they are not "the story of my life." The things that happened to me in my life have already happened, they are already formed, and time has kneaded them and given them shape. To write things as they happened means to enslave oneself to memory, which is only a minor element in the creative process. To my mind, to create means to order, sort out, and choose the words and the pace that fit the work. The materials are indeed materials from one's life, but ultimately, the creation is an independent creature.

I tried several times to write "the story of my life" in the woods after I ran away from the camp. But all my efforts were in vain. I wanted to be faithful to reality and to what really happened. But the chronicle that emerged proved to be a weak scaffolding. The result was rather meager, an unconvincing imaginary tale. The things that are most true are easily falsified.

Reality, as you know, is always stronger than the human imagination. Not only that, reality can permit itself to be unbelievable, inexplicable, out of all proportion. The created work, to my regret, cannot permit itself all that.

The reality of the Holocaust surpassed any imagination. If I remained true to the facts, no one would believe me. But the moment I chose a girl, a little older than I was at that time, I removed "the story of my life" from the mighty grip of memory and gave it over to the creative laboratory. There memory is not the only proprietor. There one needs a causal explanation, a thread to tie things together. The exceptional is permissible only if it is part of an overall structure and contributes to its understanding. I had to remove those parts which were unbelievable from "the story of my life" and present a more credible version.

When I wrote *Tzili* I was about forty years old. At that time I was interested in the possibilities of naiveness in art. Can there be a naive modern art? It seemed to me that without naiveté still found among children and old people and, to some extent, in ourselves, the work of art would be flawed. I tried to correct that flaw. God knows how successful I was.

PR: *Badenheim 1939* has been called fablelike, dreamlike, nightmarish, and so on. None of these descriptions makes the book less vexing to me. The reader is asked—pointedly, I think—to understand the transformation of a pleasant Austrian resort for Jews into a grim staging area for Jewish "relocation" to Poland as being somehow analogous to events preceding Hitler's Holocaust. At the same time your vision of Badenheim and its Jewish inhabitants is almost impulsively antic and indifferent to matters of causality. It isn't that a menacing situation develops, as it frequently does in life, without warning or logic, but that about these events you are laconic, I think, to a point of unrewarding inscrutability. Do you mind addressing my difficulties with this highly praised novel, which is perhaps your most famous book in America? What is the relation between the fictional world of *Badenheim* and historical reality?

AA: Rather clear childhood memories underlie *Badenheim 1939*. Every summer we, like all the other petit-bourgeois families, would set out for a resort. Every summer we tried to find a restful place, where people didn't gossip in the corridors, didn't confess to one another in corners, didn't interfere with you, and, of course, didn't speak Yiddish. But every summer, as though we were being spited, we were once again surrounded by Jews, and that left a bad taste in my parents' mouths, and no small amount of anger.

Many years after the Holocaust, when I came to retrace my childhood from before the Holocaust, I saw that these resorts occupied a particular place in my memories. Many faces and bodily twitches came back to life. It turned out that the grotesque was etched in, no less than the tragic. Walks in the woods and the elaborate meals brought people together in Badenheim—to speak to one another and to confess to one another. People permitted themselves not only to dress extravagantly but also to speak freely, sometimes picturesquely. Husbands occasionally lost their lovely wives, and from time to time a shot would ring out in the evening, a sharp sign of disappointed love. Of course I could arrange these precious scraps of life to stand on their own artistically. But what was I to do? Every time I tried to reconstruct those forgotten resorts, I had visions of the trains and the camps, and my most hidden childhood memories were spotted with the soot from the trains.

Fate was already hidden within those people like a mortal illness. Assimilated Jews built a structure of humanistic values and looked out on the world from it. They were certain they were no longer Jews, and that what applied to "the Jews" did not apply to them. That strange assurance made them into blind or half-blind creatures. I have always loved assimilated Jews, because that was where the Jewish character, and also, perhaps, Jewish fate, was concentrated with greatest force.

In *Badenheim* I tried to combine sights from my childhood with sights of the Holocaust. My feeling was that I had to remain faithful to both realms. That is, that I mustn't prettify the victims but rather depict them in full light, unadorned, but at the same time, that I have to point out the fate hidden within them, though they do not know it.

That is a very narrow bridge, without a railing, and it's very easy to fall off.

PR: Not until you reached Palestine, in 1946, did you come in contact with Hebrew. What effect do you think this has had on your Hebrew prose? Are you aware of any special connection between how you came to Hebrew and how you write in Hebrew?

AA: My mother tongue was German. My grandparents spoke Yiddish. Most of the inhabitants of Bukowina, where I lived as a child, were Ruthenians, and so they all spoke Ruthenian. The government was Rumanian, and everyone was required to speak that language as well. When the Second World War broke out, and I was eight, I was deported to a camp in Transmistria. After I ran away from the camp I lived among the Ukrainians, and so I learned Ukrainian. In 1944 I was liberated by the Russian Army and I worked for them as a messenger boy, and that's how I came by my knowledge of Russian. For two years, from 1944 to 1946, I wandered all over Europe and picked up other languages. When I finally reached Palestine in 1946, my head was full of tongues, but the truth of the matter is that I had no language.

I learned Hebrew by dint of much effort. It is a difficult language, severe and ascetic. Its ancient basis is the proverb from the Mishna: "Silence is a fence for wisdom." The Hebrew language taught me how to think, to be sparing with words, not to use too many adjectives, not to intervene too much, and not to interpret. I said that it "taught me." In fact, those are the demands it makes. If it weren't for Hebrew, I doubt whether I would have found my way to Judaism. Hebrew offered me the heart of the Jewish myth, its way of thinking and its beliefs, from the days of the Bible to Agnon. This is a thick strand of five thousand years of Jewish creativity, with all its rises and falls: the poetic language of the Bible, the juridical language of the Talmud, and the mystical language of the Kabala. This richness is sometimes difficult to cope with. Sometimes one is stifled by too many associations, by the multitude of worlds hidden in the single word. But never mind, those are marvelous resources. Ultimately you find in them even more than you were looking for.

Like most of the kids who came to this country as Holocaust survivors, I wanted to run away from my memories, from my Jewishness, and to build up a different image for myself. What didn't we do to change, to be tall, blond, and strong, to be *goyim*, with all the outer trappings. The Hebrew language also sounded like a gentile language to us, which is perhaps why we fell in love with it so easily.

But then something amazing happened: that very language, which we saw as a means of melting into self-forgetfulness and merging with the Israeli celebration of the land and heroism, that language tricked me and brought me, against my will, to the most secret storehouses of Judaism. Since then I haven't budged from there.

PR: Living in this society you are bombarded by news and political disputation. Yet, as a novelist, you have by and large pushed aside the Israeli daily turbulence to contemplate markedly different Jewish predicaments. What does this turbulence mean to a novelist like yourself? How does being a citizen of this self-revealing, self-asserting, self-challenging, self-legendizing society affect your writing life? Does the news-producing reality ever tempt your imagination?

AA: Your question touches on a matter which is very important to me. True, Israel is full of drama from morning to night, and there are people who are overcome by that drama to the point of inebriation. This frenetic activity isn't only the result of pressure from the outside. Jewish restlessness contributes its part. Everything is buzzing here, and dense; there's a lot of talk, the controversies rage. The Jewish *shtetl* has not disappeared.

At one time there was a strong anti-Diaspora tendency here, a recoiling from anything Jewish. Today things have changed a bit, though this country is restless and tangled up in itself, living with ups and downs. Today we have redemption, tomorrow darkness. Writers are also immersed in this tangle. The occupied territories, for example, are not only a political issue but also a literary matter.

I came here in 1946, still a boy, but burdened with life and suffering. In the daytime I worked on kibbutz farms, and at night I studied Hebrew. For many years I wandered about this feverish country, lost and lacking any orientation. I was looking for myself and for the faces of my parents, who had been lost in the Holocaust. During the 1940s one had a feeling that one was being reborn here as a Jew, and one would therefore turn out to be quite a wonder. Every utopian view produces that kind of atmosphere. Let's not forget that this was after the Holocaust. To be strong was not merely a matter of ideology. "Never again like sheep to the slaughter" thundered from loudspeakers at every corner. I very much wished to fit into that great activity and take part in the adventure of the birth of a new nation. Naively I believed that action would silence my memories, and I would flourish like the natives, free of the Jewish nightmare, but what could I do? The need, you might say the necessity, to be faithful to myself and to my childhood memories made me a distant, contemplative person. My contemplation brought me back to the region where I was born and where my parents' home stood. That is my spiritual history, and it is from there that I spin the threads.

Artistically speaking, settling back there has given me an anchorage and a perspective. I'm not obliged to rush out to meet current events and interpret them immediately. Daily events do indeed knock on every door, but they know that I don't let such agitated guests into my house.

PR: In *To the Land of the Cattails*, a Jewish woman and her grown son, the offspring of a gentile father, are journeying back to the remote Ruthenian countryside where she was born. It's the summer of 1938. The closer they get to her home the more menacing is the threat of gentile violence. The mother says to her son: "They are many, and we are few." Then you write: "The word *goy* rose up from within her. She smiled as if hearing a distant memory. Her father would sometimes, though only occasionally, use that word to indicate hopeless obtuseness."

The gentile with whom the Jews of your books seem to share their world is usually the embodiment of hopeless obtuseness and of menacing, primitive social behavior— the *goy* as drunkard, wife-beater, as the coarse, brutal semi-savage who is "not in control of himself." Though obviously there's more to be said about the non-Jewish world in those provinces where your books are set—and also about the capacity of Jews, in their own world, to be obtuse and primitive too—even a non-Jewish European would have to recognize that the power of this image over the Jewish imagination is rooted in real experience. Alternatively the *goy* is pictured as an "earthy soul... overflowing with health." *Enviable* health. As the mother in *Cattails* says of her half-gentile son, "He's not nervous like me. Other, quiet blood flows in his veins."

I'd say that it's impossible to know anything really about the Jewish imagination without investigating the place that the *goy* has occupied in the folk mythology that's been exploited, in America, at one level by comedians like Lenny Bruce and Jackie Mason, and at quite another level by Jewish novelists. American fiction's most single-minded protrait of the goy is in *The Assistant* by Bernard Malamud. The *goy* is Frank Alpine, the down-and-out thief who robs the failing grocery store of the Jew, Bober, later attempts to rape Bober's studious daughter, and eventually, in a conversion to Bober's brand of suffering Judaism, symbolically renounces *goyish* savagery. The New York Jewish hero of Saul Bellow's second novel, *The Victim*, is plagued by an alcoholic gentile misfit named Allbee, who is no less of a bum and a drifter than Alpine, even if his assault on Leventhal's hard-won compusure is intellectually more urbane. The most imposing gentile in all of Bellow's work, however, is Henderson—the self-exploring rain king who, to restore his psychic health, takes his blunted instincts off to Africa. For Bellow no less than for Appelfeld, the truly "earthy soul" is not the Jew, nor is the search to retrieve primitive energies portrayed as a quest of a Jew. For Bellow, no less than for Appelfeld, and astonishingly, for Mailer no less than for

Appelfeld—we all know that in Mailer when a man is a sadis-
tic sexual aggressor his name is Sergius O'Shaughnessy,
when he is a wife-killer his name is Stephen Rojack, and
when he is a menacing murderer he isn't Lepke Buchalter or
Gurrah Shapiro, he's Gary Gilmore.

AA: The place of the non-Jew in Jewish imagination is a
complex affair growing out of generations of Jewish fear.
Which of us dares to take up the burden of explanation? I
will hazard only a few words, something from my personal
experience.

I said fear, but the fear wasn't uniform, and it wasn't of all
gentiles. In fact, there was a sort of envy of the non-Jew
hidden in the heart of the modern Jew. The non-Jew was
frequently viewed in the Jewish imagination as a liberated
creature without ancient beliefs or social obligations, who
lived a natural life on his own soil. The Holocaust, of
course, altered somewhat the course of the Jewish imagination. In place of envy came suspicion. Those feelings which
had walked in the open descended to the underground.

Is there some stereotype of the non-Jew in the Jewish
soul? It exists, and it is frequently embodied in the word
goy, but that is an undeveloped stereotype. The Jews have
had imposed on them too many moral and religious stric-
tures to express such feelings utterly without restraint.
Among the Jews there was never the confidence to express
verbally the depths of hostility they may well have felt.
They were, for good or bad, too rational. What hostility
they permitted themselves to feel was, paradoxically,
directed at themselves.

What has preoccupied me, and continues to perturb me,
is this anti-Semitism directed at oneself, an ancient Jewish
ailment which, in modern times, has taken on various

guises. I grew up in an assimilated Jewish home where German was treasured. German was considered not only a language but also a culture, and the attitude toward German culture was virtually religious. All around us lived masses of Jews who spoke Yiddish, but in our house Yiddish was absolutely forbidden. I grew up with the feeling that anything Jewish was blemished. From my earliest childhood my gaze was directed at the beauty of non-Jews. They were blond and tall and behaved naturally. They were cultured, and when they didn't behave in a cultured fashion, at least they behaved naturally.

Our housemaid illustrated that theory well. She was pretty and buxom, and I was attached to her. She was, in my eyes, the eyes of a child, nature itself, and when she ran off with my mother's jewelry, I saw that as no more than a forgivable mistake.

From my earliest youth I was drawn to non-Jews. They fascinated me with their strangeness, their height, their aloofness. Yet the Jews seemed strange to me too. It took years to understand how much my parents had internalized all the evil they attributed to the Jew and, through them, I did too. A hard kernel of revulsion was planted within each of us.

The change took place in me when we were uprooted from our house and driven into the ghettos. Then I noticed that all the doors and windows of our non-Jewish neighbours were suddenly shut, and we walked alone in the empty streets. None of our many neighbours, with whom we had connections, was at the window when we dragged along our suitcases. I said "the change," and that isn't the entire truth. I was eight years old then, and the whole world seemed like a nightmare to me. Afterwards too, when I was separated from my parents, I didn't know why. All during the war I wandered among the Ukrainian villages, keeping my hidden secret: my Jewishness. Fortunately for me, I was blond and didn't arouse suspicion.

It took me years to draw close to the Jew within me. I had to get rid of many prejudices within me and to meet many Jews in order to find myself in them. Anti-Semitism directed at oneself was an original Jewish creation. I don't know of any other nation so flooded with self-criticism. Even after the Holocaust, Jews did not seem blameless in their own eyes. On the contrary, harsh comments were made by prominent Jews against the victims, for not protecting themselves and fighting back. The Jewish ability to internalize any critical and condemnatory remark and castigate themselves is one of the marvels of human nature.

The feeling of guilt has settled and taken refuge among all the Jews who want to reform the world, the various kinds of socialist, anarchist, but mainly among Jewish artists. Day and night the flame of that feeling produces dread, sensitivity, self-criticism, and sometimes self-destruction. In short, it isn't a particularly glorious feeling. Only one thing may be said in its favor: it harms no one except for those afflicted with it.

PR: In *The Immortal Bartfuss*, your newly translated novel, Bartfuss asks "irreverently" of his dying mistress's ex-husband: "What have we Holocaust survivors done? Has our great experience changed us at all?" This is the question with which the novel somehow engages itself on virtually every page. We sense in Bartfuss's lonely longing and regret, in his baffled effort to overcome his own remoteness, in his avidity for human contact, in his mute wanderings along the Israeli coast and his enigmatic encounters in dirty cafés, the agony that life can become in the wake of a great disaster. Of the Jewish survivors who wind up smuggling and black marketeering in Italy directly after the war, you write: "No one knew what to do with the lives that had been saved."

My last question, growing out of your preoccupation in *The Immortal Bartfuss*, is, perhaps, preposterously comprehensive, but think about it, please, and reply as you choose. From what you observed as a homeless youngster wandering in Europe after the war, and from what you've learned during four decades in Israel, do you discern distinguishing patterns in the experience of those whose lives were saved? What *have* the Holocaust survivors done, and in what ways were they ineluctably changed?

AA: True, that is the painful point of my latest book. Indirectly I tried to answer your question there. Now I'll try to expand somewhat. The Holocaust belongs to the type of enormous experience which reduces one to silence. Any utterance, any statement, any "answer" is tiny, meaningless, and occasionally ridiculous. Even the greatest of answers seems petty.

With your permission, two examples. The first is Zionism. Without doubt, life in Israel gives the survivors not only a place of refuge but also a feeling that the entire world is not evil. Though the tree has been chopped down, the root has not withered—despite everything, we continue living. Yet that satisfaction cannot take away the survivor's feeling that he or she must do something with this life that was saved. The survivors have undergone experiences that no one else has undergone, and others expect some message from them, some key to understanding the human world—a human example. But they, of course, cannot begin to fulfill the great tasks imposed upon them, so theirs are clandestine lives of flight and hiding. The trouble is that no more hiding places are available. One has a feeling of guilt that grows from year to year and becomes, as in Kafka, an accusation. The wound is too deep, and bandages won't help. Not even a bandage such as the Jewish state.

The second example is the religious stance. Paradoxically, as a gesture towards their murdered parents, not a few survivors have adopted religious faith. I know what inner struggles that paradoxical stance entails, and I respect it. But that stance is born of despair. I won't deny the truth of despair. But it's a suffocating position, a kind of Jewish monasticism and indirect self-punishment.

My book offers its survivor neither Zionist nor religious consolation. The survivor, Bartfuss, has swallowed the Holocaust whole, and he walks about with it in all his limbs. He drinks the "black milk" of the poet Paul Celan, morning, noon, and night. He has no advantage over anyone else, but he still hasn't lost his human face. That isn't a great deal, but it's something.